TOM ADAMS'
AGATHA CHRISTIE
COVER STORY

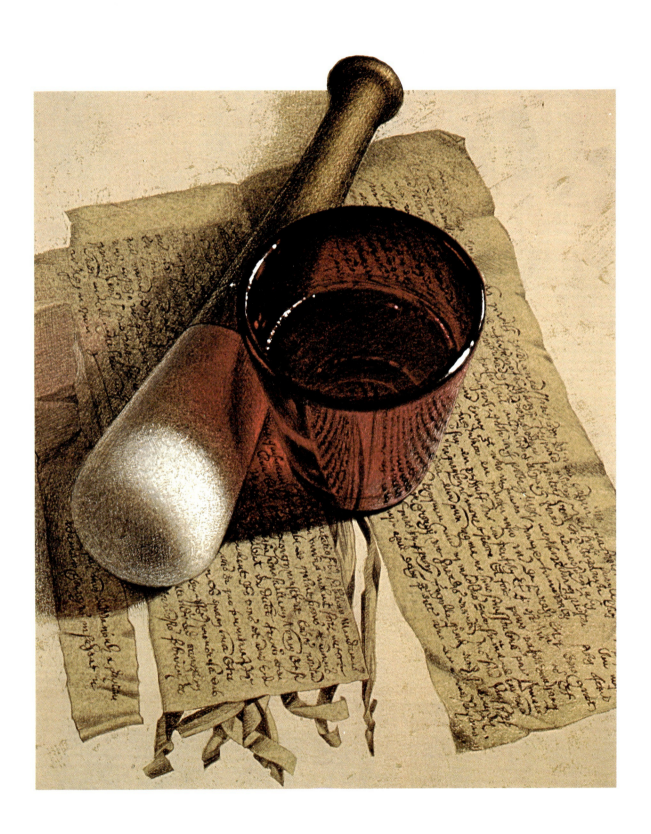

TOM ADAMS'
AGATHA CHRISTIE
COVER STORY

Commentary by Julian Symons
Introduction by John Fowles

A Dragon's World Ltd. Imprint

Dragon's World Ltd.,
Limpsfield,
Surrey RH8 0DY
Great Britain

Designed by Steve Henderson

ISBN 0 905895 62 2

Printed in Hong Kong.

CONTENTS

INTRODUCTION

BY

JOHN FOWLES

It is not only a great pleasure to introduce this now famous series of jackets, but a debt I owe the artist. Tom Adams has done cover or flyleaf illustration for four of my own five works of fiction. For the fifth I must confess that I did go to another artist—another blender of acute realism and haunting fantasy, another painstaking craftsman with a special genius for suiting image to story. I hope Tom has forgiven me this one infidelity with the 15th century master, Pisanello. I am not sure I have forgiven him for some of his work for other novelists—that quite literal dream of a jacket for David Storey's *Saville*, for example.

My first novel, *The Collector*, marked something of a turning-point in both our lives. I think Tom had done only one other jacket-painting before that year, 1962, Tony Colwell, the shrewd design director of Jonathan Cape, had decided that the book needed a jacket in the general style of the then best-known practitioner in the *trompe-l'oeil* field, Richard Chopping, who had done some celebrated Ian Fleming covers for Cape. Tom showed some characteristic doubt about whether he could bring it off, where-upon Tony Colwell promptly bet him £25 that he could. The challenge was taken; and the result was incomparably the best jacket of the year (if not of the entire decade) and was universally praised—even by rival publishers, the highest accolade there is—on

both sides of the Atlantic. I have seen dozens more jackets on other editions since and none comes within a mile of the original for beauty, subtle understatement or even sheer commercial effectiveness. It is almost as much the book to me now as my own text: inalienable from its memory.

Two years later Tom produced another remarkable cover, this time for *The Magus*. This was in his more complex and allusive style, and I remember something else about it. He kindly lent the original to me for a couple of years, but we never dared hang it. The very rich and delicate painting was done on a massive but fragile slab of dental plaster, and weighed a ton. Though Tom (despite some of the paintings in this book) is the soul of gentleness, I did not fancy the idea of having to ring him one day about a broken hook and a pile of smithereens. The book was recently re-issued with the kind of purely typographical jacket publishers have now decided is the thing for their more serious writers; and I have to answer in-dignant readers' letters demanding to know why the original Adams cover was relegated. I have lost count of those who have written saying that they originally bought the book solely on the strength of that mysterious collection of masks and flowers that Tom created.

His secret as cover-illustrator lies, it seems to me, above all in his capacity for being oblique, yet so presenting this obliquity that it constitutes a lure. As Julian Symons perceptively notes of the present series, Tom never shows violence, only its aftermath, and sometimes not even that. It is difficult to say what is menacing at all about the almost Dutch still-life cover to *The Moving Finger*: the quiet glass and the pestle sleeping on a dusty page of old legal writing. Yet even as pure picture, deprived of normal setting, it threatens. Something evil waits; and the book must be read to find out what.

Dame Agatha's heirs have not always, I understand, been too happy about some of Tom's interpretations of her stories; but he has surely matched himself to the essential secret of her work, which for me is the mixture of quiet normality and *grand guignol*, of the banal and the exotic. Sometimes he stresses the one side, sometimes the other; and again and again, in either key, with great imagination. The dead woman on the strand with the gulls is high melodrama; the drab and seemingly empty room, near bathos. Yet both work equally well.

Then there is Tom's wit, as in the pure Magritte (which Magritte himself would surely have admired) of *Murder at the Vicarage*. It may also be seen, if less obviously to the world at large, in the use he makes of his huge and magpie private collection of objects and old illustrated books. All good painters—like all good writers—infuse their work with their personal life. I was a shade anxious when I heard that Tom was going to portray the heroine of *The French Lieutenant's Woman* in his drawing for the original edition of that book. Authors rarely visualize their characters physically in any clear detail, but I had no qualms when the first proof came: it was very near indeed to what I might have come up with myself, had I been an artist. The next time I met Tom, I congratulated him on his intuitive imagination. He smiled. The head was in fact a straight portrait of his wife, whom I hadn't then met. Tom is now remarried, and I think a face beside a certain piece of driftwood in one painting here is also not from imagination.

Novels must always remain primarily their texts; and the jacket must always, I suppose, be mainly classed as a part of the selling process, the luring of the potential customer inside the covers (though only fools and the very highbrow imagine that the luring and selling stop at the printed page). Yet it seems to me that creating a good pictorial jacket for fiction—a glance in any bookseller's window on either side of the Atlantic will, alas, prove how rare an achievement this remains—is something more than the purely commercial art which is how too many publishers still view it. At its best it requires gifts beyond mere ingenuity, calculation, flair. It will show an independence of mind in the artist—an ability to hold author, text and publisher (and their often clashing demands) at arm's length, and to find a truly personal solution. I know how hard Tom has fought on occasion to keep this independence of feeling and of vision; an obstinacy that is matched in his studio by the enormous care he takes to achieve the effects he wants. I am sure he could also be a formidably good natural history painter, if he chose.

But it is time his work spoke for itself. It belongs to one of the pleasantest traditions in English art, and goes back essentially to the great woodcut school of the 1860s; and descends through Rackham, Dulac, the Detmold brothers to our own day. Tom stands honourably in that long line, and I am delighted to see a book now devoted to a man who has for so long devoted himself to the books of others. I know I speak for all past beneficiaries of that devotion when I say that he has long deserved such recognition.

John Fowles, 1979

8

FOREWORD

Confronted with the task of arranging over ninety cover paintings into some sort of coherent order several possibilities emerged. We could have arranged them in strict chronological order: interesting perhaps only in a very limited way. Style groups, such as still life, surrealist, symbolist, straight realism etc., would have been more appropriate but although I have developed several recognisable styles in the course of my career as an Agatha Christie cover artist, I was apt to revert haphazardly to earlier styles and, in any case, this would tend to be visually rather boring.

Finally, we realised that categorising them in groups of Christie themes would not only provide an opportunity for a fairly light-hearted analysis of the work of this unique writer of crime fiction but might point up some interesting visual comparisons and juxtapositions.

It is important to emphasise that these groups or categories are, in some cases, quite arbitrary. Many titles are interchangeable between one or more of the chapters. And, in fact, where there is more than one version of the same title, we have where appropriate, placed them in different chapters, ie. *Murder at the Vicarage* appears in 'Miss Marple and

Mayhem' and in 'The Darker Side of Village LIfe'. (Chapters 1 and 5).

This exercise has, at least for me, provided an interesting new insight into Agatha Christie's motives and methods as perhaps the greatest writer of whodunnit crime stories. It is possible that astute readers will find some clues in this book in that endless battle of wits with Agatha Christie but I have tried very hard not to give the game away completely.

Finding the cover paintings for reproduction in this book proved to be a task of enormous complexity. A great many of the originals are in private collections on both sides of the Atlantic; several are lost, stolen or strayed and a number of the covers are now out of print.

These problems, compounded as they were by many other vicissitudes, mainly concerning the difficulties inherent in publishing anything these days, made it virtually impossible for Julian Symons to comment on every title. In fact, twenty-four of the covers are reproduced without his wise and perceptive commentaries for which, I hope, we will be forgiven. I have tried to be as objective as possible in my own remarks. I am deeply grateful to Julian for his contribution to this book. The sharp freshness of his appraisal has in some cases been a revelation to me and, although I don't always agree with what he says, it makes fascinating reading and has added an extra dimension to the whole endeavour.

I would also like to express my gratitude to all those owners of my work who have (in most cases) been wonderfully co-operative and patient, particularly Mr. Geoffrey Greenwood who is, as you will see from the index, a very appreciative patron.

I also owe a debt of gratitude to the various and successive art directors who, over the years, have shown great restraint and appreciation; in New York, Bob Blanchard and Carol Inouye both of Pocket Books, Len Leone and Laura Glazer of Bantam; in England, Patsy Cohen, Christine Bernard, John Constable and Mike Dempsey of Fontana; in Canada, to Sharon Budd and Lucinda Vardey who, at the time of my Christie exhibition in Toronto worked so hard on my behalf, under the auspices of Collins of Canada.

A word of appreciation and gratitude must go to Mark Collins and Virgil Pomfret, the two original begetters of the Christie-Adams relationship, which I fear only marginally benefitted Agatha Christie herself but for me quite simply changed my life, and to John Fowles whose truly great novels provided the original and enduring inspiration for my career as an illustrator.

Finally, I would like to thank my wife Georgie for her expert editorial advice and Hubert Schaafsma, Steve Henderson and Karen Feldwick of Dragon's World who so lovingly mid-wifed this publication into being.

TOM ADAMS

The relevance of John Fowles' introduction to this book cannot be exaggerated. In the autumn of 1961 it was as if Tom Adams' career was to be determined by the success or failure of his cover illustration for <u>The Collector</u>. I can remember my visit to Patsy Cohen, then art-director at Collins, to show her a first proof of this cover and to suggest that Tom would be the right artist to illustrate the Agatha Christie paperback covers. She was, of course, enthusiastic about that now famous still-life, but responded in her normally cautious manner by suggesting that Tom should speculatively try one Christie cover, for <u>A Murder is Announced</u>, and, if all went well with that, others might follow.

Tom announced this particular murder agonisingly slowly. Patsy Cohen's telephone calls to ascertain progress became more frequent and increasingly sceptical. When Tom finally delivered the artwork, at the eleventh hour, all doubts were dispelled – the Adams and Christie styles were judged a perfect match. They were to be so for twenty years and few would dispute that they became the best known series of paperback covers throughout the world during that time.

Personally I owe a lot to Tom's success in those early days. In 1961 he was the first artist who agreed to be represented by me and the international demand for his work which grew rapidly opened many doors for me. More important, my enduring friendship and admiration for him has meant that I have visited his different homes many times over the years and have gained an insight into his working methods from these visits. I doubt if there has been one of these occasions when I was not made aware of something in his collection of Victoriana and bric-a-brac, that I had not seen before, that linked him even more closely to what I have often referred to as an illustrator's 'life of crime'. Numerous articles from around his home appear in the Christie cover paintings, always with an appropriateness that rejects any suggestion of an easy solution. It is, of course, part of Tom's art that he does not do anything the quick or easy way. A stickler for detail, he is seldom satisfied with any finished result and sometimes, as the observant viewer may notice, he will continue to work on a painting even after it has been printed and has appeared on the bookstalls.

Tom retires now as the Christie cover man, but his 'life of crime' continues with illustrated books of his own devising. He has recently completed <u>The Great Detectives</u> with Julian Symons and has other ideas on the drawing board. As one of the most fascinating and rewarding artists to know and work with, long may he remain at large.

Virgil Pomfret
18.vi.1981

This book is for James and Constance,
with love and gratitude.

CHAPTER ONE

MISS MARPLE & MAYHEM

"a nasty old cat"

"really Miss Marple is rather a dear"
Murder at the Vicarage

Although Miss Marple in the early stories is generally considered to be a vicious old gossip, prying and poking into everyone else's business, most people think of her in her later persona, as a very respectable and gentle old lady; very English and delightful to look at.

Her fluffy white hair, pink cheeks and china blue eyes hoodwinked most of the other characters into dismissing her as an innocent sweet old dear who wouldn't know a stilleto from a butter knife. In fact, of course, she was one of the greatest amateur sleuths of all time, leaving chief constables, detective inspectors and other professionals gasping with admiration and astonishment.

Essentially Miss Marple is the amateur *par excellence*, the quiet observer, the wise elder who solves the ultimate crime of murder by reference to the peccadillos and petty failings of character found in ordinary village life.

But perhaps the most interesting characteristic of Miss Marple is the fact that she is not quite what she seems. The most innocent people have their sinister aspects and there is surely something chillingly sinister about a frail old lady homing in unmercifully on criminals' secrets, cutting through the smokescreen of lies and duplicity like a laser beam. What an uncomfortable neighbour she would make!

Having rejected, as Julian Symons points out elsewhere in this book, the option of portraying Miss Marple or Hercule Poirot figuratively, I have attempted, (and this applies to a large number of my Christie cover paintings) to portray that oddly addictive innocent/sinister paradox by the manner in which I paint objects and symbols, giving them a kind of hallucinatory intensity which seems to suggest, perhaps, that beneath the flawless exterior there might be something rotten and evil.

This section contains my first and last Christie painting. *A Murder is Announced* was painted in 1962 and *Miss Marple's Final Cases* in 1980, a span of eighteen years. It is generally accepted that Agatha Christie's classic period is from 1920 when her first book, *The Mysterious Affair at Styles* was published, to the early fifties. This is not to say that she wrote no masterpieces after that period—in fact *The Mirror Crack'd* and *At Bertram's Hotel* are excellent stories, written in the sixties. But the early classics, *A Murder is Announced*, *Murder at the Vicarage*, *The Moving Finger* and *The Body in the Library* all take place in typical English rural surroundings and are vintage Christie.

A MURDER IS ANNOUNCED

JULIAN SYMONS

The conventional cover for a detective story, whether by Agatha Christie or another writer, is likely to show some scene such as a man being hit on the head, or running down a dark alley, or discarding a pair of bloodstained gloves . . . the variations of subject are endless, but the style does not vary very much.

From the beginning Tom Adams's covers for Agatha Christie's books broke with this convention. He read the book three times, first of all very quickly, then making notes of characters or incidents, then with a direct view to ideas for illustration. He found up to half-a-dozen ideas, tried one or more of them out, and in the end found something that satisfied him artistically and also echoed something in the book. But he went further than this, rejecting immediately the idea of showing Poirot or Miss Marple. The rejection was instinctive, but later on he rationalised it, with the argument that both characters were so firmly fixed in the reader's imagination that they could never be satisfactorily shown. Partly true, no doubt, but my guess is that the rejection was based on the fact that as

subjects they didn't greatly stir his imagination. He thought there were more interesting things to be done.

What were they? This is the first Adams cover. It is a straightforward still life, a scene from the book, clock on mantelpiece, violets in vase, bullet holes in wallpaper. The cutting from the local paper is the only intrusion on realism. There is a *trompe-l'oeil* effect created by the wallpaper background contrasted with the clock and violets, which was to be developed much further. A very individual, very unusual book cover—although not many people noticed that at the time.

TOM ADAMS

I have a soft spot for this first Christie cover painting, although I now feel it to be one of those I place in my personal category of early primitives. The newspaper clipping in particular is not very convincing.

The painting took rather a long time to do; I was nervously aware of how much my future depended on its reception. In fact, it pleased both Mark Collins and Betsy Cohen, at that time jointly responsible for Fontana covers. I remember clearly my happy feeling of relief as I basked in their approval.

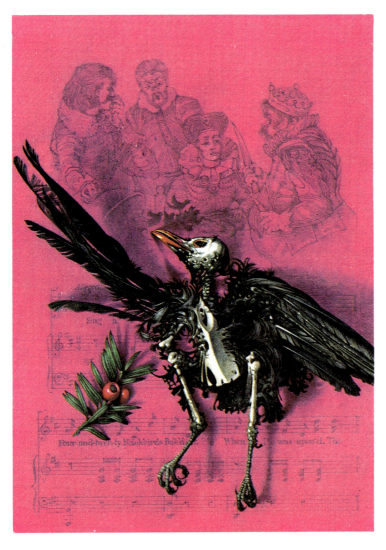

▲ A POCKET FULL OF RYE

JULIAN SYMONS
The use of poisons occurs in 54 Agatha Christie books. They range from cyanide (used 14 times), morphine (7) and digitalis preparations (6) to such rarities as taxine poisoning, suffered by rich man Rex Fortescue here. "*Most* unusual. Really delightfully unusual", says the doctor. In the dead man's jacket was found a pocket full of rye, and later in the book a maid is found strangled, with a clothes peg pinned to her nose. ("Down came a blackbird and picked off her nose.") The cover rightly concentrates on the nursery rhyme. It provides a decorative background, and there is the blackbird, which was painted from a rotting skeleton. The result has the right Christie flavour: It is basically decorous, but with the decorum goes a strong suggestion of something nasty.

TOM ADAMS
I am irredeemably addicted to the collecting of skulls and skeletons, sometime, I am afraid, even before the flesh has decently departed from the bones. My family think the habit morbid and unattractive.

This cover is the first example of a formula I used often. A simple, two dimensional drawing washed with colour providing a background for a more or less *trompe-l'oeil* painting of objects.

THE 4.50 FROM PADDINGTON ▶ (U.S.) WHAT MRS. McGILLICUDDY SAW

JULIAN SYMONS
In all the Tom Adams covers for Christie books there is not a single scene showing violent action. The temptation must have been strong here, for the opening chapter describes a murder very vividly, as Mrs. McGillicuddy sees it committed through the lighted window of a train running parallel with hers. "His hands were round the throat of a woman who faced him, and he was slowly, remorselessly, strangling her." The scene would have been an obvious choice for illustration to most artists. But not for Adams. His feeling that this would have been wrong, both for him ("I'm not that kind of artist"), and the books, is undoubtedly right. Murder may be seen taking place, but violence of a physical kind is not a vital element of the story. So Tom Adams is true, both to himself and his author, in producing a highly formal cover, with the clues—a sprig of flower, a piece of fur, a compact—in the foreground, and behind them the romantic and impressive Roman sarcophagus in which a body was found.
This is one of the more cunning Christie confections, and the artist clearly felt the need to exercise restraint.

TOM ADAMS
A restraint slightly marred by the fact that this painting contains one of my occasional howlers. I did this illustration in early spring and so delighted was I to have a piece of hawthorn blossom to paint I forgot to check the season of the story. The murders were committed in winter; those little white flowers have been mocking me ever since.

Tom Adams '67

17

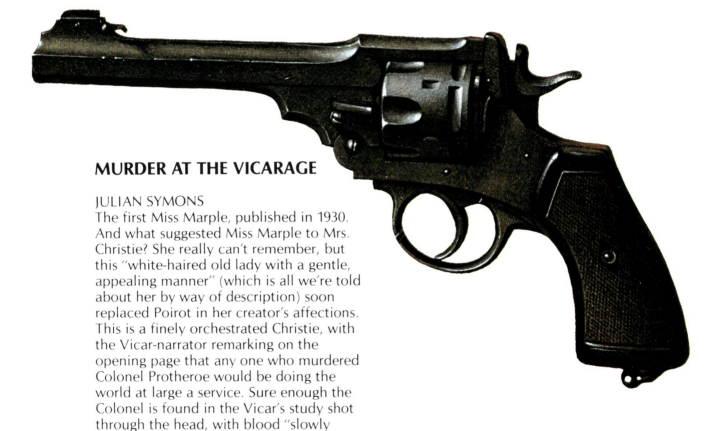

MURDER AT THE VICARAGE

JULIAN SYMONS
The first Miss Marple, published in 1930.
And what suggested Miss Marple to Mrs.
Christie? She really can't remember, but
this "white-haired old lady with a gentle,
appealing manner" (which is all we're told
about her by way of description) soon
replaced Poirot in her creator's affections.
This is a finely orchestrated Christie, with
the Vicar-narrator remarking on the
opening page that any one who murdered
Colonel Protheroe would be doing the
world at large a service. Sure enough the
Colonel is found in the Vicar's study shot
through the head, with blood "slowly
dripping on to the floor . . . drip, drip,
drip." The story has been cunningly devised
to suggest a similarity to the trick used in
The Murder of Roger Ackroyd, but Miss
Marple finds a quite different solution.

All the items on the shelf in this early
still life play a part in the story, the books
beneath are a touch of artistic licence.
Pointless to complain that the effect is
static (what else can a still life be?), but
somehow it seems to me that the items on
the shelf don't carry quite the menace they
should.

TOM ADAMS
Julian is quite right about this cover, the
third of the early primitives and totally
without menace. I hadn't learnt to paint
guns at this stage and it is, generally
speaking, an untidy and unresolved
conglomeration. Authenticity was my
obsession. The tube of paint for instance,
belonged to my grandfather and hadn't
been opened since the thirties before I
sacrificed it for this cover. And that is a
contemporary Collins 'Crime Club' novel
under the Baedeker.

THE MOVING FINGER ◀

JULIAN SYMONS
In this early still life the artist was, I think, deliberately avoiding the obvious. The story is about anonymous letters made of words cut from newspapers, so he shows — an old legal document. There is a death from cyanide, and we get an innocent glass of water. Another murder is committed with a kitchen skewer sharpened to a fine point, but we are given instead the pestle used to stun the victim. The composition is effective, but I didn't feel the book had much engaged the artist's interest.

TOM ADAMS
I think I can justifiably claim not to have been quite so obscure as Julian suggests. It is very rash of him to assume that any glass of water appearing in one of my covers is innocent. This is one of those paintings where I have provided an extra clue which . . . but no, I won't spoil it—read the book carefully and all will be revealed.

I vividly recall the pleasure I derived from painting the very simple still life and the challenge of keeping the beautiful script lying flat on the parchment. The document comes from an interesting volume of Record Office facsimiles in my possession.

NEMESIS ▶

TOM ADAMS
This is by way of being a sequel to *The Caribbean Mystery* in which Miss Marple, accepting a posthumous challenge from Mr. Jason Rafiel, a character in that earlier story, ends up in Jocelyn St. Mary. Here nemesis, in the person of Miss Marple, duly exacts its revenge. It contains (unusually for Agatha Christie) a strong suggestion of sexual deviation in the plot.

The collapsing greenhouse and the camellia come from the camellia house at Chiswick House, London. Someone might even recognise the silhouette of the tree.

▲ AT BERTRAM'S HOTEL

JULIAN SYMONS
One of the interesting things about the Adams covers is that, although all are painted, some offer an almost photographic naturalism. The façade of Bertram's Hotel is rendered meticulously from that of a famous London hotel known and loved by Americans, and it's done with the accuracy of a photograph. So why not use a photograph? Because then you would get a different effect, probably one much less sinister. What we have is Bertram's Hotel, immensely respectable, and posed against it elements in the story, a poisoned chocolate and a bullet held like a cigarette in a woman's hand. This works better than any similar photographic conjunction or opposition could possibly do.

TOM ADAMS
Surely the hand and bullet are more photo-graphic than the hotel which in fact is quite graphically treated. However, it will hardly come as a surprise that I agree with Symons' remark about the inadequacy of photography as a medium for the illustration of fiction. A savagely cropped cover; we have lost the top of Bertram's Hotel and the bottom of the hand. Unfortunately, we were unable to reproduce this from the original for various reasons and so had to resort to the latest published version.

THE MIRROR CRACK'D FROM ▶ SIDE TO SIDE

JULIAN SYMONS
Out flew the web and floated wide;
The mirror crack'd from side to side;
'The curse is come upon me', cried
The Lady of Shalott.
The figure here is taken from an actual Victorian drawing of Tennyson's Lady of Shalott, and although the device of the break in the mirror cutting the picture has been used in other covers for the book, it has never been done so imaginatively. The contrast between the delicacy of the foreground figure and that bloodstained staring eye, together with the web delicately suggested by what may be waving curtains, produces an image of disquiet that becomes more powerful the longer you look at it. For some strange reason the artist himself was disappointed with this marvellous cover.

TOM ADAMS
I really am at a loss to know why this cover is so much liked. Julian Symons is not alone in his opinion. The original is owned by that splendid illustrator and designer, Jan Pienkowski and whilst I am quite prepared to agree it is a cracking good idea, I would love the chance to re-do this one day.

I think my chief disappointment is with the quality of the painting itself and that it does not do justice to that neglected but excellent Victorian painter, J.W. Waterhouse, from whom I borrowed the lady.

Tom Adams
'62

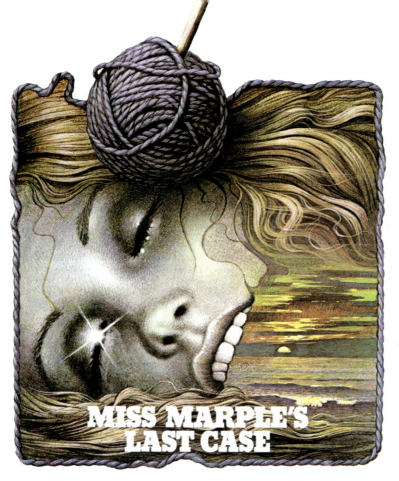

MISS MARPLE'S LAST CASE

▲ SLEEPING MURDER

JULIAN SYMONS
The last Miss Marple, or at least the last *published* Miss Marple, for in fact the book was written many years before publication. Like the Poirot *Curtain* it was designed to appear after the author's death. It is one of several Christie tales that move back into the past, as Gwenda from New Zealand is oppressed by odd feelings about the house she has bought (something of the author's interest in houses goes into Gwenda's arrangement of the furniture). Then a visit to the theatre to see *The Duchess of Malfi* overwhelms Gwenda, when she hears the play's most famous line: "Cover her face. Mine eyes dazzle. She died young," and we are away on the scent of an old crime with the refusal to let sleeping murder lie.

Not a great deal of this gets into a painting that slightly disappointed me. Needles and a ball of wool are nicely symbolic of Miss Marple, but I seem to have seen that dead girl in other covers. Not every story strikes off sparks in an artist, and I didn't feel a strong electrical impulse flowing here.

TOM ADAMS
It is true I am perhaps over partial to those horizontal girls, but who's complaining? In fact, the wool and the knitting needles were demanded by Mark Collins as, I imagine, a kind of memorial to Miss Marple. My scope in doing this was limited by the largely typographical design of this special paperback.

THEY DO IT WITH MIRRORS ▶ (U.S.) MURDER WITH MIRRORS

JULIAN SYMONS
"And that, you see, is how the conjuring trick was done. It was the trick of the lady sawn in half that made me think of it."

So far Miss Marple, and not another explanatory word must be said here. Agatha Christie's tricks with mirrors were dazzling, and this brilliant cover plays similar tricks. It is one of my half-dozen favourites among the whole collection of Tom Adams covers.

TOM ADAMS
The trick of the landscape sawn in half: a fine story to illustrate. A real gun on a real sheet of music placed against real mirrors. The whole assemblage arranged one fine summer day, in a real garden on the Isle of Wight. You can't beat that combination. I hope I did it justice.

MISS MARPLE'S FINAL CASES ◀

TOM ADAMS
A posthumous collection of short stories, containing some previously published only in the United States. This is the last cover I painted for Fontana.

THE BODY IN THE LIBRARY ▶
(European version)

JULIAN SYMONS
"The more Americans there are, the more people there are reading *The Body in the Library*," Emma Lathen wrote, and probably she picked this title because a dead body in a library typifies for many the archetypal Christie story. In fact Agatha Christie's themes are as various as her methods of murder, and my guess would be that she chose this title quite deliberately, and also deliberately introduced the body on the second page. It is found by a housemaid, and Colonel Bantry is told about it by his butler.

The author, in fact, was ever so gently guying the form she was using. For Tom, it was one of those books where he felt inclined to work against the grain. "Where the title could be illustrated in a straightforward way I avoided it", he says, and in the English version he avoids it brilliantly, with that dazzling impression of a beaded dress. He is taking a slight liberty with the book's evening dress of "white spangled satin", but one forgives him for the charm of the composition.

TOM ADAMS
Sometimes I do stretch a point, conveying impressions rather than reality. And, quite frankly, those beads are not quite 'white spangled satin', and the foot is shoeless. But I couldn't resist the combination of sparkling beads and black fur, foot and flies. Incidentally, the flies reappear several times on my covers, perhaps rather obvious symbols of Death and Decay but I am very fond of insects.

CHAPTER TWO
POIROT & POISON

"In the little grey cells of the brain
lies the solution of every mystery"
Hercule Poirot

"Foreigners, you can't trust foreigners,
not even if they *are* hand-in-glove
with the police"
Death in the Clouds

If Miss Marple is the amateur sleuth *par excellence*, then Hercule Poirot, ex-Belgian policeman and recognised expert on poisons, is the real professional. He is subtle, even cunning, and utterly ruthless. Nevertheless, behind that incredibly neat *petit bourgeois* exterior, beats a romantic heart. He was frequently very sympathetic to star-crossed lovers, often helping and encouraging them with perception and kindness. He dearly loved his great friend Captain Hastings, even while being intensely irritated at his obstinate stupidity.

His extreme conceit and personal vanity were more a way of 'psyching' the opposition than actual vices. Like a pocket-sized Mohammed Ali, he almost seemed to court amused contempt — an attitude his enemies eventually came to regret of course.

Agatha Christie was a great admirer of Conan Doyle and, in the relationship of Poirot with his rather thick-headed but intensely loyal friend Hastings, she was paying homage to the Holmes-Watson partnership, even introducing the heavy-handed policeman, Inspector Japp as an equivalent for Inspector Lestrade.

In his expertise on poison, Poirot was merely reflecting his creator's own experience in a dispensary during the First World War where, as a V.A.D. nurse, Agatha Christie acquired some extremely esoteric knowledge of poison, not only of the more conventional ones like arsenic and strychnine but also some really way out substances like, Evipan, used in *Cards on the Table*; Dispholidus Typus venom (extracted from the Boomslang snake) in *Death in the Clouds*; strophanthin in *Murder in the Mews* — all three in this section; coniine in *Five Little Pigs* and gelsemium in *The Big Four*. He was involved in no less than forty cases of poisoning in his long career.

The length of Poirot's career is an interesting problem in itself. When the *New York Times* printed Poirot's obituary notice, his age, it was implied, must be at least 120! This absurd contention has been nicely dealt with by Julian Symons in his biographical studies, *The Great Detectives*. Many other interesting facts about Poirot's somewhat mysterious origins are revealed therein, culled from the memoirs of Captain Arthur Hastings, O.B.E.

Even though she herself regretted his popularity and very soon became bored with him, the brilliance of Agatha Christie's creation of this strange, eccentric little figure, with his flamboyant posturings is seen, I believe, in the perfect foil he makes to the Englishness of her plots and characters. The English have always been convinced of how vastly superior they are to all those dreadful foreigners and so it was a stroke of genius to turn the tables on them in the guise of a little Belgian.

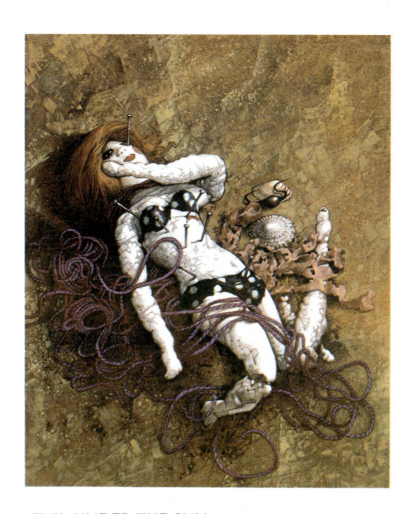

EVIL UNDER THE SUN
(English version)

TOM ADAMS
The doll for this painting was modelled in wax by a young friend who was working for me at the time. He very much enjoyed painting and sticking pins in it. As can be seen from the sand background, this was painted at a time when I was trying to develop a more painterly quality in my work. For artists the road to perfection, which in itself is a mirage, has many seductive but dead-end side tracks like this.

EVIL UNDER THE SUN
(U.S. version)

JULIAN SYMONS
"When a sexually carnivorous young woman
appears on the Christie scene, the reader,
recognising the stock figure of the home
wrecker, needs no further inducement to
trip down the garden path to self-deception."
The acute comment about this book is by
Emma Lathen. Here is the sexual carnivore,
here is the boat from which the rowers
jumped to find the body . . . and here in
the foreground is a piece of driftwood,
curiously appropriate although it finds no
place in the story. Its meaning? "Pure
symbolism . . . a piece of self-indulgence",
the artist says. He liked the shape, and so
do I.

TOM ADAMS
Self-indulgence; yes, but there is more to it
than that. The piece of driftwood was the
first and most beautiful present from
someone I had just met at the time I was
painting the cover. The clue to who it was
lies elsewhere in this book.

jewels accreted on the bee's legs instead of pollen. This is a compendium image, a device I used several times for short story collections.

THREE ACT TRAGEDY ▶
(U.S.) MURDER IN THREE ACTS

JULIAN SYMONS
Or, as you might say, a three card trick, with a nicotine-laced cocktail as the deadly ace of spades. Stephen Babbington, a harmless clergyman with absolutely no enemies, takes a cocktail before dinner ("I think that my wife will allow me to have one", he says with a gentle laugh) and is dead within minutes. As Hercule Poirot discovers, none of the other guests could have been sure that Babbington would take the poisoned drink. Was somebody else the intended victim?

This has always seemed to me a much underrated book. Its deliberately theatrical quality is not accidental, and the baffling puzzle is in some ways a trial run for *The ABC Murders*. The Adams cover is a most accomplished piece of painting, but it doesn't have much to do with the book. Come on now, Tom, own up!

TOM ADAMS
I shall own up to an important error in this painting but not to the main charge—that my painting is irrelevant. The glass in question is not Stephen Babbington's cocktail glass, but Sir Bartholomew Strange's port glass. Both the poisoned glass of port (responsible for the death of Sir Bartholomew Strange) and the rose (the poison used is nicotine, an alkaloid extracted from a rose spraying solution) either directly or indirectly relate to the story.

But here I humbly admit my grave error. It is fundamental to the murder technique that the glasses used to administer the poison were *cut* glasses and mine is a plain port glass.

▲ POIROT'S EARLY CASES

JULIAN SYMONS
"No, but seriously, *have* you ever failed?" "Innumerable times, my friend. What would you? *La bonne chance*, it cannot always be on your side."

And Poirot goes on to tell Hastings the story although, as one might guess, the "failure" looks very much like a success. Some of these early stories contain ingenious tricks, and all have a verve that compensates for the occasional debt to Conan Doyle. Fans will be pleased by one of the rare appearances of Poirot's secretary, Miss Lemon.

Tom Adams's cover refers to a story involving death by an apparent bee-sting. "Give me a chance to draw an insect and I take it", he says. The head I take to be that of the intended youthful victim. A gruesome, effective combination.

TOM ADAMS
Actually the head is that of a puppet which appears in one of the stories, as do the

THE HOLLOW

JULIAN SYMONS
The most imaginative and compelling of the early covers. The design is simple. A revolver has been dropped into a pool, a few bubbles show on the surface, a single leaf suggests that summer is over. Nothing more. Yet those few elements, and somehow especially the rising bubbles, convey someting disquieting, something *wrong*, about the relationships in the agreeable Angkatell family.

TOM ADAMS
I had a lot of fun and a great deal of trouble with this cover. It was painted in those innocent days when having a firearm certificate in England meant no more than being on good terms with one's local police sergeant. Needless to say I have long since been stripped of this dubious privilege and so have to draw or photograph guns on the premises of a theatrical hire shop, or use replicas.

▲ PERIL AT END HOUSE

JULIAN SYMONS
This is one of my favourite Christies, generally underrated by critics. Here Poirot shows in his full glory, caustic and comic by turn, full of vanity but brilliantly intelligent. It is one of the books that makes me regret Tom Adams's self-imposed ordinance about not depicting Poirot. A pilot, a plane fuselage, the flames indicating the plane being shot down — where do they appear in the story? The answer is that they don't, although they do prompt the action. The World War I Luger has its place in the tale, and the cover is a nice geometric design.

TOM ADAMS
It is one of my favourites; I suppose partly because of my love of anything to do with old aircraft, and indeed this obsession of mine may have influenced me unduly in my choice of subject matter. But I don't think so. One of Agatha Christie's characteristic ploys is the use she makes of long dead incidents from which spring the actual events related in the story. The ancient grievance nursed over the years, the mental unbalance brought about by an obsession with something real or imagined that happened a long time ago; frequently in childhood. Surely one of the key threads running through this story is a lament for the long lost hero-lover.

Moreover since almost every Christie story has an English setting one jumps at the chance of getting away from it.

DEATH IN THE CLOUDS ▶ (U.S.) DEATH IN THE AIR

JULIAN SYMONS
This is an unusually direct illustration, even though the gigantic wasp has, in an artistic sense, surrealist origins. Eleven passengers are on a plane from Le Bourget to Croydon (the book, which appeared in 1935, has a nice period flavour in relation to air travel), and one is killed. She has a mark on her neck, and a wasp has been flying around in the cabin. Was the wasp responsible, how did it get there? Below one passenger's seat is a curare-tipped thorn, and the blowpipe that might have been used is found under the seat of . . . Poirot. A Christie classic, a splendidly appropriate cover.

TOM ADAMS
As I explain in my note on the English version of *Mrs. McGinty's Dead*, the effect may be surrealist but it's really only the ultimate in optical perspective. The small object fills the eye and it is the artist's privilege to be able to depict both this and the far objects in sharp focus and thus indulge in perceptual confusion. Flying must have been a joy in the glorious Imperial Airways Hengist but alas, another howler — the name of the plane in the story is Prometheus — goodness knows how I overlooked this. In fact, for someone who was so obsessed with authenticity, I made an uncomfortable number of mistakes over the years. At least I got the period right.

THE LABOURS OF HERCULES

JULIAN SYMONS
"They had long curved noses, like birds . . . over their shoulders they wore loose cloaks that flapped in the wind like the wings of two big birds." These are two of the characters, but what a horrific image the artist has made of them. Again Adams has succeeded in bringing his own sense of the macabre into an orthodox short detective story.

TOM ADAMS
Nice chance to play with the classic myth and try to give it a modern twist. The sinister shapes and patterns of feathers and wings have always intrigued me. Also I like painting apples—most artists do.

39

CARDS ON THE TABLE

JULIAN SYMONS
Mr. Shaitana, a wealthy dilettante, is stabbed to death during an evening at bridge. The story is deliberately artificial (four undetected murders and four detectives are the guests), and the cover is suitably formalised. The card table; two hands of cards; the four suits and the four players. An an imaginative work this cover is not on the same level as those for *A Caribbean Mystery* and *Destination Unknown*, but as a clever rendering of the murder situation it is one of the best of all. Poirot was one of the bridge players, by the way, so one of those eyes, or one pair of lips, must belong to him. I fancy the diamond eye myself.

TOM ADAMS
There is a marvellously dramatic picture by John Collier called 'The Cheat' showing four people playing bridge at the moment of frozen amazement when it is discovered that one of the ladies is actually cheating! I extracted elements from this Edwardian horror picture for part of this cover painting.

MURDER IN THE MEWS
(U.S.) DEAD MAN'S MIRROR

TOM ADAMS
Four excellent stories. A mirror, one of
Agatha Christie's favourite devices comes
into one of them and the Egyptian God of
Death, Anubis, whose shadow appears in
Death Comes as the End, is reflected in it.

   A great many of these early Christie
covers (and this is not one of my favourites)
seem to be a bit gory. I can only excuse
this excess on the grounds that I was egged
on by Mark Collins; but we did enjoy
ourselves.

AFTER THE FUNERAL
(U.S.) FUNERALS ARE FATAL
(U.S. version)

TOM ADAMS
Murder in the family circle: archetypal
Christie with a painting of Polflexan
Harbour and wax flowers under a glass
shade as major clues. I used a Victorian
painting of a nun and several paintings of
West Country harbours—a favourite subject
of Victorian painters as reference for this
cover.

LORD EDGEWARE DIES
(U.S.) THIRTEEN AT DINNER

TOM ADAMS

An oddball Christie story this one—an unpleasant peer who gets his come-uppance; the Poirot-Hastings-Japp trio operating in London's high-society.

It could be claimed that this painting represents my one major departure from a self-imposed rule about depicting images of violence. Although not a violent action in itself, an explicit close-up like this may be too close for comfort. It was the subject of fierce argument between Mark Collins who loved it and Christine Bernard, the art director, who hated it.

I think a *grand-guignol* image like this is just bearable if, as I hope I have succeeded in doing, the artist gives it a kind of dream-like quality. The dagger is, in fact, a Victorian paper knife.

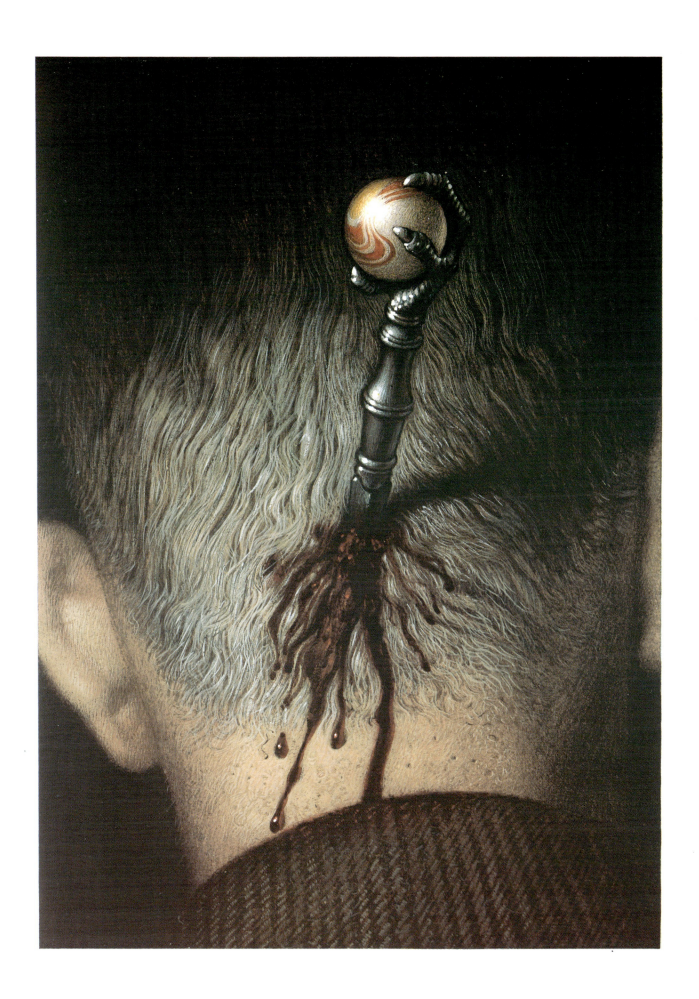

HICKORY DICKORY DOCK

(U.S. version)

JULIAN SYMONS
I much prefer the effective realism of this,
the American, cover to the English version
in Chapter 4. Here, the realism is suffused
with poetic feeling by the street lamp, and
the lights in the pub windows set against
the slightly sinister foreground figures.

TOM ADAMS
I also much prefer this interpretation. I
really feel I distilled the mood of the
incident which inspired it. The other
painting, reproduced in Chapter 4, is rather
contrived.

SAD CYPRUS

TOM ADAMS
This is a love story and one of the accepted great classics. It has, unusually for Christie, a courtroom drama. The poison is morphine and the author uses her expert knowledge in this field to good effect.

The photo in the picture is based on one of my father taken during the First World War and I tried with the simplest elements to reflect the air of emotional fatalism which seems to run through this story. I also think the title is one of the most evocative of all Agatha Christie's.

CHAPTER THREE
SINS OF THE FATHERS

"Amongst everyone's ancestors there
has been violence and evil"
Five Little Pigs

This is the smallest category but in some ways the most important, in conjunction with 'Something Nasty in the Nursery'.

Christie was, above all else, a believer in the family. She says in her autobiography that she values loyalty above all other virtues. Loyalty and courage. Nevertheless, she had her share of family troubles and if you are looking for evil and cruelty in its subtlest forms, the family is where you will find them.

In these stories, there is an assortment of inherited feuds, real or imagined grievances between sisters and brothers, fathers, sons and daughters; sometimes sibling jealousy as in *Death Comes as the End* or filial resentment as in *Hercule Poirot's Christmas*.

The typical plot is a family gathering — perhaps seasonal. A member of the family dies and mutual suspicion is passed uneasily like the parcel in that well-known children's game, shedding one wrapping after another until, lo and behold! the unhappy culprit is revealed. Sometimes even knowing who is and who is not a member of the family is quite difficult — but an essential ingredient in the search for the murderer. In one case, I

won't say which, the family murder turns out to be a complete red herring.

In two books in this category, another twist of the family tale is apparent; the feeling of responsibility of one 'good' member for another 'bad' member's criminal actions. The protective instinct for the less fortunate, perhaps tainted member of the family, even to the point of 'justifiable homicide' becomes a compelling motive.

A very powerful element in Agatha Christie's personality which deeply suffuses these stories is her concern with Evil as an Entity. Sometimes this Entity takes the form of international plots; 'The Brain' behind revolutionary movements: Chapters 6 and 7 include a number of this type. However, much more credibly, it is the conflict of Good and Evil within the village, the family and even within the individual. I think Christie strongly conceived one of her roles to be that of moralist; her genius lies however, in the fact that she never forgot that her primary function and strength lay in her role as entertainer, even though the moral message is there, plain for all to see.

TAKEN AT THE FLOOD
(U.S.) THERE IS A TIDE

JULIAN SYMONS
I don't think any of the covers conveys better than this one the sense of the artist's increasing assurance, his sense that he can mix disparate elements with the feeling that they will either explain themselves, or that readers are prepared to accept the deliberately strange juxtapositions. Here are rescue workers (Gordon Cloade, rich man, is killed in the blitz), a lipstick (the shape suggests an unexploded bomb to the artist, although if I were looking for symbolism I should be more nearly reminded of a penis), red lips (courtesy of Marilyn Monroe), and fire tongs. all have a place in the story. The general redness is London burning. Each element is rendered realistically, yet the total effect is strongly symbolic. As to the relationship of cover to book that must be called symbolic too, since although the story does start in the blitz, almost all of it takes place in 1946, after the war.

TOM ADAMS
Here I think Julian Symons is a little hard on me. Although what he says is true about the main action in the book, the early blitz incident I take to be pivotal to the whole story. As to the lipstick, have it your own way Julian, you may well be right.

THE CROOKED HOUSE
(U.S. version)

JULIAN SYMONS
in her autobiography Agatha Christie says
that places have always been more real and
memorable to her than people. The shape
of a hill, she says, can be wrong, a house
may be in the wrong place, and she
expresses this feeling in the novel *Crooked
House*:

> "*I wondered why it had been called
> Three Gables. Eleven Gables would have
> been more apposite! The curious thing
> was that it had a strange air of being
> distorted . . . It was like looking at a
> country cottage through a gigantic
> magnifying-glass. The slantwise beams,
> the half-timbering, the gables—it was a
> little crooked house that had grown like
> a mushroom in the night!*"

And there it is, meticulously created, in
Tom Adams's American cover. Tom says
himself that it is a piece of strict realism,
but I should call the cover strongly romantic,
with the three figures placed beautifully for
the maximum of sinister, enigmatic effect.
The English still-life is effective too, with
pills and ballet shoes elements in the story,
but the American cover catches my own
sense of the book's macabre quality.

TOM ADAMS
A mish-mash of various quite well-known
English houses. The head is that of Mary
Dunning, my wife at the time this painting
was done and the girl comes from an
Arthur Rackham illustration.

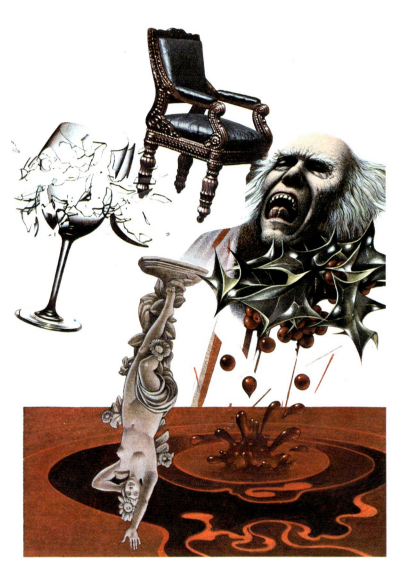

HERCULE POIROT'S CHRISTMAS (U.S.) MURDER FOR CHRISTMAS

JULIAN SYMONS
The artist took his cue from the writer's dedication, in which she said that she was responding to her brother-in-law's wish for "a good violent murder with lots of blood". So blood is all around wretched old Simeon Lee, who has had his throat cut. Blood drips from the holly, even the berries are turning to blood drops that form a spreading pool. And yet (this is the real achievement, I think) both paintings have a sort of Christmas jollity about them. In one, everything is so crowded that every inch of the picture is busy, so that it might be a Victorian Christmas. At a guess I should say that this picture had its origins in a Victorian *genre* painting. In the other screaming Simeon, shattered wine glass, floating chair, inverted statue, might all be part of a childish romp. In these two pictures the artist is clearly having fun.

TOM ADAMS
For some reason the earlier version of this was disliked by the Christie family and in response to their wishes another version was commissioned. I enjoyed doing both but I prefer the first one. To be strictly accurate these are the second and third versions of the book. The first one is not included.

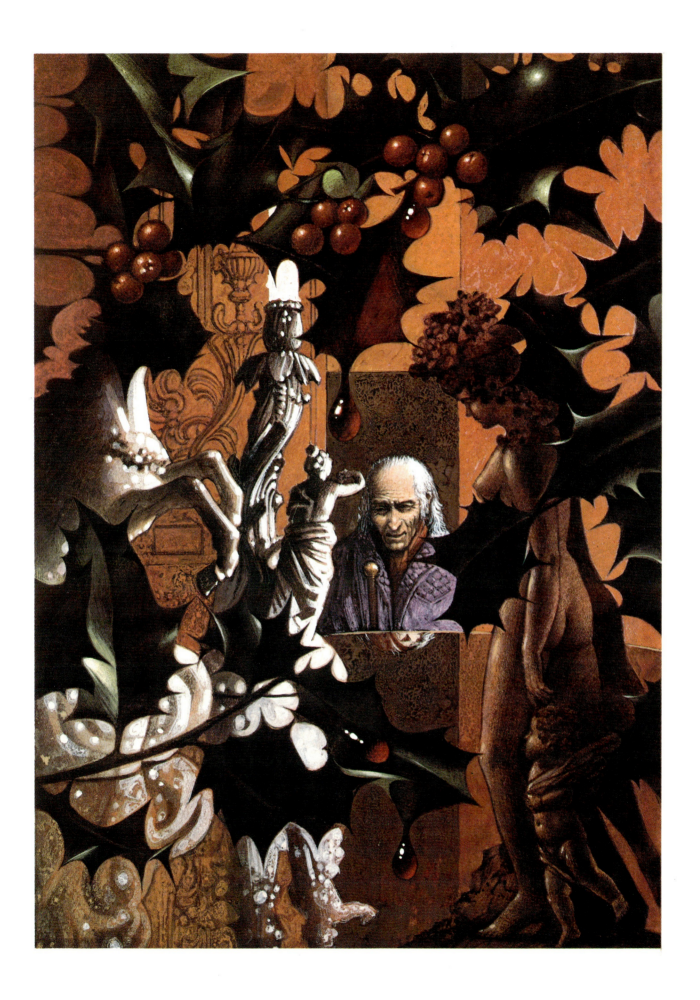

◀ ELEPHANTS CAN REMEMBER

JULIAN SYMONS

As Agatha Christie grew older (this book appeared in 1972) she inclined more and more to use plots involving research into the past. So here the Christie *alter ego*, Ariadne Oliver, finds herself digging into a twenty year old crime, as a result of questions asked her at a literary lunch. "You write these wonderful stories, you know all about crime", says her nosey and unpleasant questioner. But Mrs. Oliver can't remember. . . .

This is a very engaging opening to a consistently enjoyable and alert story, one of the best late Christies. Tom's painting embodies elements in the plot, and makes a charming, teasing composition. I particularly liked the spectral remembering elephant brooding over that slightly desolate marine view.

TOM ADAMS

This painting is quite recent and I like it very much—it is my idea of the really successful book cover. It combines mystery, appeal and the sinister in balanced proportions, and says everything about the story without giving anything away. Many people will recognise the dog as being cribbed from Landseer but perhaps an echo of one of my favourite paintings, *The Scape Goat* by William Holman Hunt will also be detected.

ORDEAL BY INNOCENCE ▶

JULIAN SYMONS

This is one of the most tantalising of later Christie's (no Poirot or Miss Marple), the tale of a man who discovers that he has been responsible for a miscarriage of justice, and causes emotional havoc when he tries to explain the reasons. The painting, technically I think one of the finest in the book, is symbolic and mysterious. It is the black bird of ill omen that is ravaged, the bird of peace that has blood on its claws. . . .

TOM ADAMS

Unfortunately, Julian only saw one of these paintings, because here is the complete set of four different but related interpretations

of this title.

Sometimes I found the title as intriguing as the story, and in this case the title could probably go on triggering images in my mind for ever. The earliest is the simple broken cup still-life, the fighting birds the latest; a span of about twelve years between them. The corridor in the American version was inspired by a Jonathan Miller television production of *Alice in Wonderland*.

ORDEAL BY INNOCENCE

DEATH COMES AS THE END
(European version)

JULIAN SYMONS
One of Agatha Christie's experiments, giving the lie to those who say that all of her books are really the same. Characters and plot come from two or three Egyptian letters of the XI Dynasty, and the action takes place about 2000 B.C. The characterisation may have been rather twentieth century, but the author took great trouble over the details. How was meat cooked? Did men and women eat together? At a table, or on the floor? Was linen kept in chests or cupboards? What were the houses like? The book is unique also in the fact that she gave way to an expert adviser about the ending, and always regretted doing so. "I still think now, when I re-read the book, that I would like to re-write the end."

Agatha Christie's concerns have a great deal of relevance to the cover, which has the hieratic formal feeling, and the interest in detail, at which the author aimed in the book. Were all the background details right for the period? If they had been seriously inaccurate, I am sure that Tom Adams would have heard from Agatha Christie.

TOM ADAMS
This is an early cover and I am afraid the background wall painting *is* historically inaccurate. I regret this but I must have been carried away by the beauty of this particular mural and the fact that the girl's profile in it was so remarkable similar to the friend who posed for me wearing Egyptian style makeup.

In both versions I simulated the dishevelled mummy wrappings with bandages soaked in a strange concoction of mud, paint, candle wax and ointment and arranged them as they might have looked, if distrubed by a contemporary tomb robber. This painting was for the European cover. The American version is in Chapter 6.

CHAPTER FOUR

SOMETHING NASTY IN THE NURSERY

*"The root of a person's actions lies
in his genetic make up"*
Hallowe'en Party

There are two basic themes running through this category. First, of course, children; children as victims—children as villains: and they are the privileged children of the well-to-do middle classes, not the little unwashed savages of the gutter. One expects and excuses primitive behaviour on their part but what about a blood-stained Christopher Robin?

The second theme is the nursery rhyme. The nursery is the sacred temple of middle class childhood and nursery rhymes are its hymns. Seven of these books have nursery rhymes as titles or minor themes and, in some of them that is about all they have to do with the plot.

Clearly Agatha Christie was attached to these ancient traditional songs and it is not hard to see why. Quite apart from her obvious liking for something so much a part of her own happy childhood, there is the paradoxical strain of violence and cruelty and thinly veiled references to tragic historical events which run through British nursery rhymes like a scarlet thread. They fit her stories like a glove and I am immensely grateful to her for providing me with ready-made ideas for cover paintings which exactly suit my constant search for equivalents and symbols.

There are sombre themes here of inherited insanity and deep frustration and yet this section contains Agatha Christie at her best as an entertaining teller of tales—*Crooked House* (one of her own favourites), *And Then There Were None* and *Five Little Pigs*, all masterpieces, but especially *Five Little Pigs*, considered by many to be her best, a real *tour-de-force* with a characterisation and subtlety of perception which rises well above her usual level. And for an artist, this story is particularly pleasing. There are signs of a real appreciation of the power of the visual art of painting.

HICKORY DICKORY DOCK

JULIAN SYMONS

"The visual disturbances set up a mental disturbance, and that's what I'm always trying for", the artist says with particular reference to this cover. That's all very well, but when you compare the picture with the story—which is about a student hostel, young men and women, mysterious thefts, kleptomania, murder—the only link between them is the diamond ring. The painting *is* disturbing, but I thought also self-indulgent, at least in the European version.

TOM ADAMS

I suppose I must admit to stretching things a bit far on this one but on the other hand a very frightened girl, the mouse, (which ran up the clock) and the diamond are all important elements in the story and the mouse's feet are irresistable don't you think?

This painting had to be reproduced from film and shows the unfortunate results of 'cropping'. This is a disease from which most art directors suffer. It can strike them down at any time in their careers. I have known quite young designers, fresh out of art school, already quite badly infected. In its early stages the symptoms are a mostly unnecessary but harmless trimming off at the edges, but when the disease becomes chronic as in this case, the results are weird. Eyes can be sliced through and strange excrescences develop. Very sad.

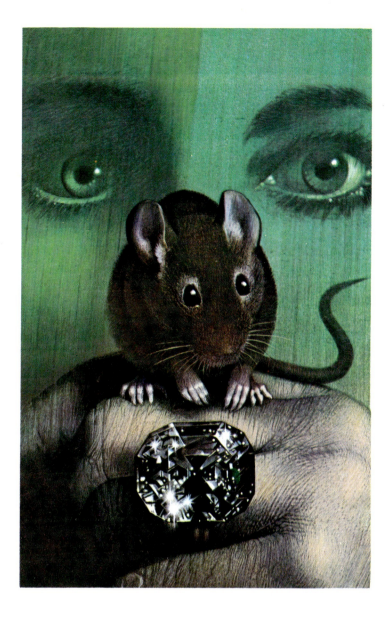

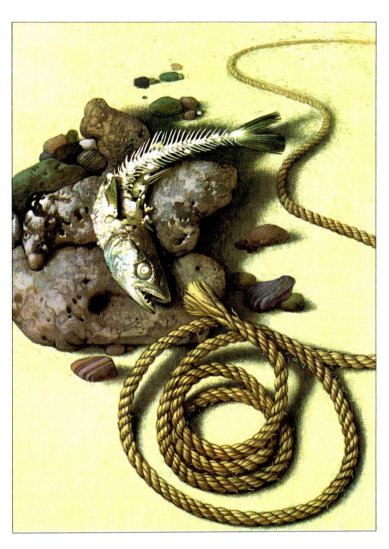

◄ TOWARDS ZERO ►

JULIAN SYMONS
This is a detective puzzle, plus a study in abnormal psychology. The artist could have used many details from the story, a golf club, red and blonde hairs on a coat, an old-fashioned steel fender. He went for something more direct, although with a touch of symbolism too. I think he's the person to explain it.

TOM ADAMS
The story contains among other things an epic swim and both the rope and the rotting fish appear in it. In the European version the rope is coiled into a "zero" and the fishes head curves "towards zero". This is not in the least significant as far as the story is concerned merely one of the little games I sometimes play in my covers; readers may or may not notice these things; it is quite unimportant whether they do or not.

Yes I did paint the fish from "life" but you will no doubt be relieved to know that it was over-cooked rather than over-ripe.

The American cover is merely another symbolic variation. Like Hockney and other artists, I find the distorting effect of water fascinating.

N OR M?

JULIAN SYMONS
One of the very cleverest covers. Nothing new in the use of the jigsaw form, but the cunning with which several disparate elements in this light-hearted spy story are introduced can only be appreciated after reading the book. This is one of the paintings that shows most clearly the ingenuity and thoughtfulness of the artist's approach.

TOM ADAMS
One of the nursery rhyme themes again. Tommy and Tuppence 'doing their bit' in wartime Britain. I think allowances should be made for the fact that it was written in 1940-41.

If I had the chance to do this one again, I should try to project the missing jigsaw pieces with shadows. I played games with this design—perhaps you have already noticed.

Within the illustration: HE FOUND A CROOKED SIXPENCE UPON A CROOKED STILE ... HE BOU... AND THEY ALL LIVED IN A CROOKED LITTLE ...

THE CROOKED HOUSE
(European version)

TOM ADAMS
The original of this painting is one of those listed in the back of the book as missing and is reproduced here in the only way now possible, from film separations. Unfortunately the original has been 'cropped'.

POSTERN OF FATE

JULIAN SYMONS
There are Christie devotees who love the
Tommy and Tuppence stories, and she herself
found these light-hearted characters
imposing less strain on her than Poirot, or
even Miss Marple. Their constant flippancy
grates on me like a file scratching glass,
and I found them no more congenial than
usual here, as they stumble over an old trail
of poisoning and spying, than I did when
they first appeared more than half a
century earlier in *The Secret Adversary*.
However . . .

But, I am full of admiration for Tom's
painting, and happily record that he liked
the book much more than I did. A nice
nostalgic feel about it, he said. The decayed
greenhouse in the painting comes into the
story, the slightly surrealist treatment of it
evokes the past, and the rocking horse is
found in the greenhouse. "Mathilde . . . a
rather splendid-looking horse even in
decay." She makes a splendidly dramatic
cover too.

TOM ADAMS
As often happens, my preferences in Christie
stories depend more on whether they stir
my visual imagination than on the more
dispassionately assessed criteria applied by
Julian. I am a sucker for nursery nostalgia
and there is lots of it here. Any book with
old greenhouses and rocking horses
immediately lowers my defences. In this
cover, I painted the decaying greenhouse
from life in my own garden and the rocking
horse belonged to the son of a great friend.
In fact, this picture echoes one of the very
first oil paintings I ever did of my own
rocking horse, sadly now no more.

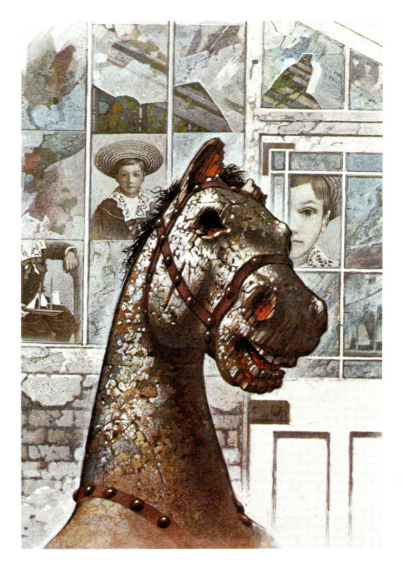

AND THEN THERE WERE NONE

JULIAN SYMONS
"When the sea goes down, there will come
from the mainland boats and men. And
they will find ten dead bodies and an
unsolved problem on Indian Island."

Those are the last lines of *And Then
There Were None*, alias *Ten Little Niggers*,
alias *Ten Little Indians*. This is one of the
two or three most famous books, and
rightly so, for it is a real marvel of plot, the
kind of puzzle which one never tires of
studying. "It was so difficult to do that the
idea had fascinated me", the author herself
said, and any reader is likely to be
outguessed, spotting the likely murderer
early on, nodding in self-satisfaction as the

characters are whittled down from ten to
two, with his suspect one of them. And
then. . . .

As often where the plot is extremely
complex, the artist has moved towards
simplicity. The rope, the seaweed, the figure
among the rocks, make a satisfying pattern,
although this is not one of my favourite
covers.

TOM ADAMS
I much prefer the European cover for this
superb story. I borrowed the doll from a
local shop. I have been accused of giving
too much away in this picture. I don't think
so; you would have to be a clairvoyant to
spot anything helpful.

AND THEN THERE WERE NONE
(U.S. version)

▲ ENDLESS NIGHT

JULIAN SYMONS
Some are born to Sweet Delight,
Some are born to Endless Night.
As Agatha Christie entered her last decade she became more concerned with the question of inherited evil. She expressed herself positively in her autobiography as being in favour of killing the incurably sick or totally anti-social, and in one or two of the later books the idea of the psychopathic personality is firmly confronted.

Endless Night takes Blake's lines as title in dealing with such a personality, and although I can't agree with the reviewer who said that this was her most devastating surprise ending, there is an unusual strain of strong feeling in the story. The artist's task was to find a pictorial equivalent of this feeling, and the solution he reached

was simple and excellent. A vignetted background suggests Gipsy's Acre, where the narrator and his wife come to live; in the foreground is the dead bird, which they find skewered with a knife that pins a small piece of paper containing a threatening message. The skewered bird on its back, pathetic but also in its implications sinister, catches perfectly the sombre tone of the book.

TOM ADAMS
One of the best of late Christies in my opinion.

The book was bought, I imagine at great expense, by *The Saturday Evening Post*, (the original *Saturday Evening Post*) and serialised in America before publication in the U.K. Asger Jerrild, the then art director of the 'Post' came over to London and commissioned me to illustrate it.

I wanted to do something rather special and as I was living in London at the time with little access to dead birds I rang up the R.S.P.C.A. just on the off-chance that they might have something. I was told that they had just been given the corpse of a Tawny owl which had died in mysterious circumstances without a mark on it. A night bird! This was too good a chance to miss.

With great reluctance and a strange sense of doing something wrong I arranged the body and stabbed that lovely plumage in the name of realism.

FIVE LITTLE PIGS ▶
(U.S.) MURDER IN RETROSPECT

JULIAN SYMONS
A good many Christie plot devices are verbal, a matter of a name or phrase misheard, or used with some special meaning. So it is here. Read the book carefully, consider the picture described in Chapter 7, and you may solve the puzzle,

But verbal clues must be the despair of an illustrator. So the artist has embodied elements of the story to make a charming composition.

TOM ADAMS
Late nineteenth century illustration was the source of inspiration here.

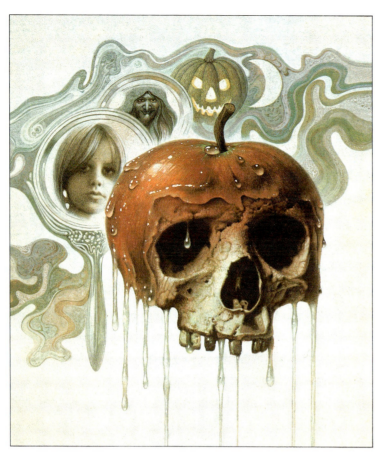

basic image from life. I photographed an apple under running water and combined it with the same skull I had used in *The Hound of Death*.

ONE TWO BUCKLE MY SHOE ▶ (U.S.) THE PATRIOTIC MURDERS

JULIAN SYMONS
There were all sorts of possibilities for illustration in this story, which begins with Poirot in the dentist's chair ("a trace of decay on that upper molar"), goes on to the dentist's apparent suicide, and continues with the horrific death of Miss Searle, face battered out of recognition, and on her foot a shabby shoe with an ornate buckle, that provides a clue in the puzzle and also, incidentally, the title.

Did the artist reject the shoe and buckle, the unrecognisable face, the dental chart, as too obvious? Perhaps. This beautifully painted nursery rhyme background with the gun pointing through has a symbolic quality. The horrors of reality are breaking through into the nursery rhyme, nursery tea, Christie world.

TOM ADAMS
An early cover, one of the first to use a nursery rhyme as background, in this case, with the foreground object breaking through from behind the background. This cover also demonstrates another variation of the sinister/pretty paradox; it could be called the collision of opposites. Sometimes simple contrast as in moth and gun (*The Mysterious Mr. Quin*), sometimes a mixture of revolting and pretty as in *A Pocket Full of Rye* or combination images like the juicy apple/ desiccated skull of *Halowe'en Party*.

▲ HALLOWE'EN PARTY

JULIAN SYMONS
The party is for teenagers, bobbing for apples is part of the fun. Thirteen year old Joyce tells crime writer Ariadne Oliver (generally taken to be an Agatha Christie self-portrait) that she saw a murder once long ago, but didn't understand that it was one at the time. During the party somebody holds Joyce's head down in the bucket where she was bending down to bob for apples. No wonder Ariadne says: "I never want to see an apple again."

The element of strangeness, Tom Adams says, is what he tried to bring to the Christie stories, equivalents of reality rather than a literal rendering of it. So the apple becomes a skull, the pumpkin menaces, water drops from and surrounds the girl and the witch. Splendid equivalents these, catching the feeling of the story and adding something to it as well.

TOM ADAMS
This is one of those happy but rare occasions when I was able to paint my

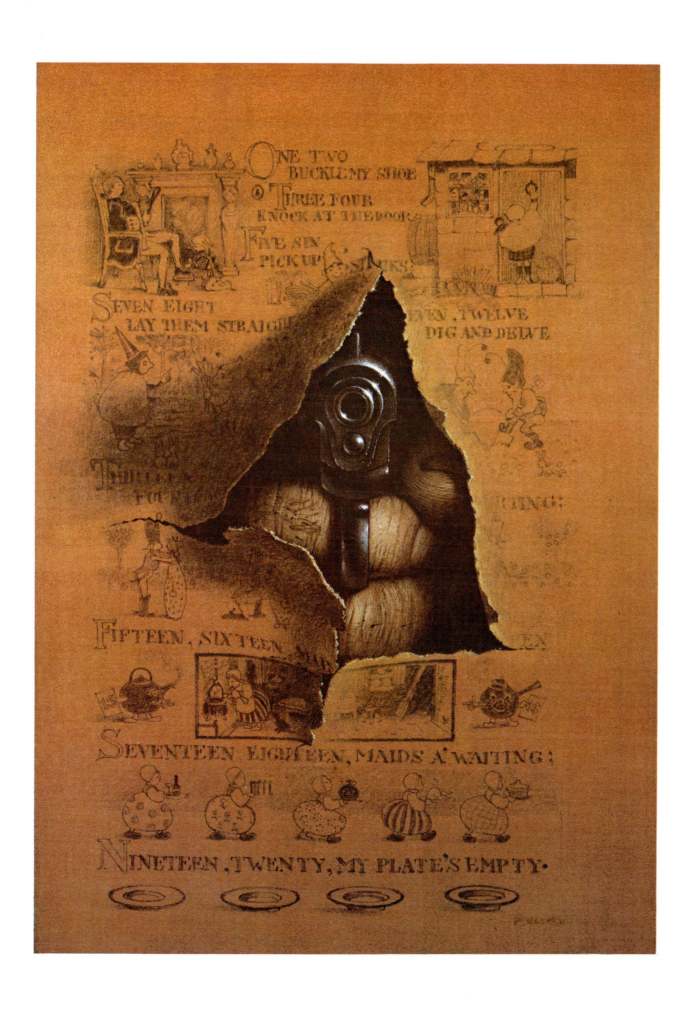

BY THE PRICKING OF MY THUMBS

JULIAN SYMONS
The story has a macabre quality fully realised in the European and American covers. The child's doll in the European cover, which has been retrieved from a chimney, is described as having lost one of its eyes, but it is the artist who has provided those sinsister cracks on cheek and forehead.

TOM ADAMS
Variations on a theme; the head comes from the second version. The first was rejected by John Constable, art director of Fontana, because it didn't meet his strict stipulation that there should be only one central object against a vignetted background for the special 'first time in paperback' format; a quite justifiable criticism.

CHAPTER FIVE

THE DARKER SIDE OF VILLAGE LIFE

"There is a great deal of wickedness in
village life"
The Thirteen Problems

"It is my belief Watson, founded upon my
experience, that the lowest and vilest alleys
in London do not present a more dreadful
record of sin than does the smiling
and beautiful countryside"
Sherlock Holmes

With the publishing of *The Murder of Roger Ackroyd* in 1926, Agatha Christie achieved two major breakthroughs in the history of crime writing. The story itself, considered by many experts to be her best, broke with convention in its ingenious, even outrageous plot and established her, in the eyes of a confused but on the whole delighted public, as a really great writer of crime fiction. The second breakthrough was to move crime from the predominantly urban world which had hitherto been its milieu, to the quiet backwaters of the English village. And this, as with the nursery theme, would seem to personify the real secret of Agatha Christie. The eternal paradox of evil behind a pretty surface.

So we happily exchange the explicit violence of the city for the gentle tinkling of a lethal cup of tea, the faint plop of a poison letter on the hall carpet and the twitching of lace curtains, behind which lurks the darker side of village life. And there is the occasionally added spice of the occult as in *The Pale Horse* and *The Sittaford Mystery*.

The village itself is rarely described in detail or located accurately. Sittaford is on Dartmoor but most of the villages in this section are only vaguely West Country in character. The names are evocative; Broad Hinny, Wychford-under-Ashe, Kings Abbott, Nassecombe, Much Deeping and Miss Marple's home village of St. Mary Mead, of which there is at least a sketch map in *Murder at the Vicarage*.

They are cardboard cut out villages in

many ways, as far as their physical aspects are concerned and, indeed, this criticism can be levelled at the characters. The squire up at the Manor, the vicar, the doctor, the local shopkeepers; all are slightly obvious caricatures rather than profound character studies. But to criticise Agatha Christie for this is to miss the point. It is the plot that counts. The secret passions, suspicion, hatred, envy and greed; the behaviour patterns emerging from the interaction of these elements are acutely observed and lovingly drawn.

One of the fascinating things about Agatha Christie is that for every highbrow who disapproves of her, it is possible to find one of equal calibre who admires her—not, it is true, for her literary abilities but for her amazing feats of conjuring and deception, her ability to serve up murder with the Spode and silver of an English country house teaparty and make it as deliciously acceptable as a cucumber sandwich.

There is a change over the years, of course; council houses and workers' estates are built, and ugly new buildings out of character with their surroundings like the Wychford Village Institute in *Murder is Easy*. As early as 1931 in *The Sittaford Mystery* a reference is made to six bungalows built by Captain Trevelyan as a speculation; neat, identical and probably quite horrible in appearance, utterly ruining a small Dartmoor hamlet.

The element of snobbery must also be noted. The Christie world is middle middle to upper middle class. Class consciousness is still undoubtedly a strange and destructive force in Britain, one of the root causes of our economic problems no doubt, but it exists in most countries in some form or another. Perhaps it is because the British species of class structure is more complex and subtle that it engenders such amusement and contempt. However, Agatha Christie writes with a fair amount of healthy realism and self-knowledge about her own class and is quite capable of using her readers' easy assumptions about her supposed attitudes to trip them up.

Is it possible that we take a guilty pleasure in a way of life which is outmoded, riddled with social injustice but lit by an addictive glow of nostalgia?

MURDER IS EASY
(U.S.) EASY TO KILL

JULIAN SYMONS
Tom Adams sees the English landscape
romantically, and his interpretation of it is
often sinister. In the English cover that
background of green with the dead tree
standing out against it with something that
looks like an eye in the centre of it, is
uncommonly menacing. The symbols in
the foreground; that agonised face, the
nobly horned head, the cock with its red
comb signifying blood and suggesting
sacrifice (a dabbler in black magic enters
the story, and curious things happen in
Witches' Meadow), all combine to create a
sense of something unpleasant. And there
are several unpleasant characters, a bigger
ration than usual, in this book.

The American cover, equally good in its
way, avoids these atmospherics and
concentrates instead on showing us several
elements in the story. Misleading elements,
Tom admits, red herrings "which I enjoy
doing sometimes". And again, there are
more red herrings than usual in this tale,
although there are also perfectly good
clues that may suggest the mass murderer's
identity. Consider carefully, for example,
the precise words of Miss Pinkerton in the
opening chapter about the murderer . . .

TOM ADAMS
The second (English version) is not quite
such a red herring as the first. I will say no
more.

MURDER IS EASY

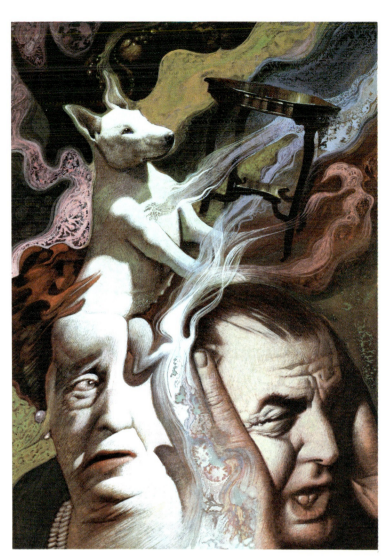

◄ THE SITTAFORD MYSTERY ► (U.S.) MURDER AT HAZELMOOR

JULIAN SYMONS
The tiny Dartmoor village of Sittaford snowed up, a table rapping seance at which a death taking place six miles away at Exhampton is announced, these are some of the story's elements and characters. The cover (second version) is not one of my favourites, but it is cunningly designed to tell you a lot without giving anything away.

TOM ADAMS
Here I had a fascinating time minutely characterizing all the protagonists, not something I do often, but I could not resist it—they were such a nasty lot.

The character in the middle was, I regret to say, murdered by one of my ancestors.

The first version is an interesting but not entirely successful blending of disparate objects.

DEAD MAN'S FOLLY

JULIAN SYMONS
Surely this (the European version) is one of the most beautiful paintings in the whole collection, suffused with a poetic feeling in part pre-Raphaelite, in part macabre. Some artistic licence has been taken. The Greek temple of which we see the pillar is real enough, but the real girl wasn't wearing a Girl Guide's uniform, although she was a guide, and the body was found in a boathouse and not a daisy-strewn field. But none of this matters when the painting is as fine as that done by Tom Adams here.

What about the book? It begins with Ariadne Oliver arranging an up-to-date version of the old fashioned game of Murder, feeling worried about something she can't specify, asking Poirot's help. The game, predictably, turns into reality. The plot is too artificial for this to be called Grade One Christie, but it's a teasing puzzle.

TOM ADAMS
I enjoyed painting both versions of this cover. I can't think why I was so lax in my attention to detail in the English version but I did occasionally (as with the Fontana version of *The Body in the Library*) allow the spirit rather than the letter of the story to guide me.

DEAD MAN'S FOLLY | (U.S. version)

MURDER AT THE VICARAGE

JULIAN SYMONS
What I like particularly about the cover
was not so much the Magritte-like tennis
racket head, ingenious though that is, but
the way in which the artist has blended
elements of the story (the racket, the letter
and the girl in the wood all enter it) with a
design that symbolises the decorous
country-vicarage-village-street atmosphere
of the tale.

TOM ADAMS
I refer to my occasional cribbing from
great masters like Magritte in my
comments on *Destination Unknown* but it
might be of interest to know that the
tennis racket is a nice piece of authentic
realism. The Dunlop people kindly lent me
one of the early rackets in their archive
collection as reference. The shape was in
the process of changing to the more familiar
modern silhouette at the time the book
was published in 1930.

MRS. McGINTY'S DEAD

JULIAN SYMONS
"Seldom was there any appreciation of subtlety", Poirot reflects. "Scenes of violence and crude brutality were the fashion, and as a former police officer, Poirot was bored by brutality." He recalls the McGinty case as being boring in this way. "It had not been an interesting murder. Some wretched old woman knocked on the head for a few pounds. All part of the senseless brutality of these days."

In this book Agatha Christie might have been offering a challenge: *Take the most commonplace crime you like, give it to me and I will make something exciting from it.* And she does. Tom Adams has sensed all this. His covers, English and American, are determinedly realistic. Here is the parlour of Mrs. McGinty, an ordinary charwoman, with the remains of her supper, kipper, bread and margarine as described in the book. It is the typical parlour of an English cottage, ornaments, pictures, oil lamp on the table. Only the ubiquitous fly, the Adams mark of death you might say, disturbs the scene's everyday quality. And by giving us this direct realism the artist has produced covers remarkably tuned to the feeling of the book.

TOM ADAMS
I revelled in the little cameo setting for the demise of Mrs. McGinty. As my main reference for these paintings I used a police photograph, reproduced in a book by J.D. Casswell Q.C., of the actual scene of a murder which was remarkably similar in circumstance to the story of Mrs. McGinty. I didn't really intend the fly to look like a science fiction monster, it is merely exaggerated perspective.

Although the parlour interior is better painted in the American version, I rather prefer the earlier one.

MRS. McGINTY'S DEAD (U.S. version)

THE PALE HORSE (U.S. version)

TOM ADAMS

This tale starts for a change in the trendy world of the Chelsea coffee-bar set of the early sixties. It soon moves down to the country, however, and becomes involved in some very sinister goings on in Much Deeping.

Ariadne Oliver (*alter ego* of Agatha Christie) is present, together with several other characters from previous books. I took the easy path and played with the black magic element—perhaps I should have been less obvious.

My working technique is quite simple if laborious. I first rough out the composition and transfer it to either an illustration board for inks and gouache or a gesso panel for oil and acrylic.

I work up the whole thing tonally to the finest detail in pencil and apply a fixative. This method is open to criticism as it inhibits freedom of development at a later stage. But my Christie illustrations do tend to be more cerebral than most of my other work.

I gradually build up transparent layers or washes of inks, acrylics or oils, establishing the broad colour balance and reinforcing the pencil drawing with very dark paint.

Sometimes at this point I apply a very thin varnish to bring up the darks and kill absorption, but this has to be done with extreme care and is probably only necessary on paper surfaces. By this time the pencil work will have almost disappeared.

The penultimate stage is building up the light areas with acrylic or gouache. I frequently use the "tonking" method to achieve certain effects or to control the thickness of paint. "Tonking", so called after the late Professor Tonks of The Slade School, means the laying of paper over the wet paint, rubbing down and pulling off, leaving only a thin layer of textured or modified paint.

Finally I work up the light areas and add the highlights.

THE MURDER OF ROGER ACKROYD

JULIAN SYMONS
"Ackroyd was sitting as I had left him, in the arm-chair before the fire. His head had fallen sideways, and clearly visible, just below the collar of his coat, was a shining piece of twisted metalwork."

A scene, indeed a crucial scene, in what is for me as for many others, upon the whole the finest Christie. "A narrow, tapering blade, and a hilt of elaborately intertwined metals of curious and careful workmanship", had been plunged into Ackroyd's back. In the story we are told specifically that it was a Tunisian dagger, and Tom Adams was lucky enough to find one. The result is a remarkable cover.

TOM ADAMS
This cover took rather too long to paint. Trying to follow the intricate and beautiful workmanship of filigree and inlaid silver nearly drove me to distraction. In my obsessive concern for realism I actually plunger the dagger through my own tweed coat on a dummy; the only way to find out exactly what happens to cloth when you strike a dagger through it in anger. With the addition of a little red ink and the forerunner of the flies that were to hover around several of my later illustrations, I set the grisly scene.

This is a partner to *Lord Edgeware Dies* but although I went to elaborate lengths to achieve realism, the fact that there is no actual flesh visible, somehow makes it a more acceptable image and one of my favourites.

THE BODY IN THE LIBRARY
(U.S. version)

JULIAN SYMONS
Here is Colonel Bantry in his library and
there's the body, or at least legs and shoes.
Trying to analyse the reasons for my
admiration of this painting, I think they lie
in the contrast between that meticulously-
painted background, realistic yet so stylised
that there is something deliberately artificial
about it (is that bookcase real, or is it a
false front concealing a secret passage?),
and the intrusion of the rug and the two
feet in the foreground. How easy and
obvious it would have been to show the
whole body—and how much better not to
do so.

TOM ADAMS
I was obliged as Julian says to be more
realistic, so I decided to go the whole hog
and do what Agatha Christie herself did—
echo the faintly ludicrous and archetypal
image conjured up by the story title.

104

CHAPTER SIX

OUT & ABOUT WITH MURDER

"Next morning I rushed round to Cook's,
cancelled my tickets for the West Indies and
instead got tickets and reservations for a
journey on The Simplon-Orient
Express to Stamboul . . ."

"Trains have always been one of my
favourite things . . ."
Agatha Christie *An Autobiography*

I respond warmly to Agatha Christie's feelings about trains—six of the books in this section feature them, more or less prominently. The fact that in one of her best books, *Murder on the Orient Express* the entire action takes place on a steam driven train and in one of her worst books, *Passenger to Frankfurt* the jet plane figures prominently, says it all. Travel is not what it used to be.

In this section are many of those Christie stories in which we are taken away from the English village and travel by various routes from the English South Coast in *ABC Murders* via The Blue Train and The Orient Express—as passengers to Frankfurt, Syria, Iraq, Egypt and The Caribbean—to an unknown destination in the desert and even, at last, back in time by 4000 years when *Death Comes as the End*.

As most Christie fans are aware, her second marriage was to Sir Max Mallowan, the distinguished archaeologist and authority on Assyrian Culture. It was natural, therefore, that some of the stories should be set in those parts of the Middle East where she travelled with her husband and lived for some time.

There is another, not so successful, element in this group of books. The subject of world-wide conspiracy and international crime as mentioned in Chapter 3. This was a genre which Agatha Christie should have left strictly alone. To be successful in this field

one has to camp it up like Dornford Yates or Ian Fleming, or be brutally realistic and professional like John Le Carré or Len Deighton. She, and indeed poor Hercule Poirot, were way out of their depth in *The Big Four* for instance, and one can see all the worst aspects of her class, the chauvinism and a rather hysterical paranoia about the Socialist menace to "civilisation as we know it".

Fortunately for us Christie soon left this type of story behind and concentrated on her true metier, only occasionally giving in to temptation with books like *N or M?* (Chapters 4 and 7), *Destination Unknown* and *Passenger to Frankfurt*.

Nevertheless, in spite of her simplistic theories and attitudes which tend to make some of the stories in this section rather ridiculous, one is aware of her essential goodness of heart and an endearing desire to disseminate joy. This positive, forward-looking side of her nature is best seen in her feelings about war and the future. She says something quite astute in her autobiography: "The time of the tigers is over; now, no doubt, we shall have the time of the rogues and the charlatans, of the thieves, the rotters and pickpockets; but that is better—it is a stage on the upward way." The fact that the tigers are back with a vengeance does not subtract from the wisdom of this observation made in 1965.

THE ABC MURDERS

JULIAN SYMONS

This is one of the masterpieces, a perfect marvel of plot. Mrs. Archer is killed in Andover, Betty Barnard in Bexhill. Is a mad murderer going through the alphabet? One of the problems for an illustrator must have been the impossibility of giving away any direct details without spoiling the story. Clues couldn't be shown, because there are no clues of an ordinary kind in the tale, only deductions. Tom Adams set out to find equivalents for the *frisson* of horror you get from the tale, and succeeded brilliantly. The ABC Railway Guide (courtesy of British Rail archives) is a perfect frame for the Magritte-like image of beach and girl. "An ABC open at the trains to Bexhill was found actually under the body", Poirot tells Hastings. The American cover presents the same scene with a more straightforward romanticism. The herring gull is a powerful image, presaging the further death ahead.

TOM ADAMS

I have painted well over a hundred illustrations for Christie covers and, of course, have not always managed to achieve the treble goal of illustrating the story, interpreting the mood and producing a good painting. I think the American version of *The ABC Murders* scores on all three counts. I am glad that I pulled it off for one of Agatha Christie's very best stories.

For the European version, I enjoyed tracking down the appropriate ABC Railway Guide; it took some doing but research into authentic background detail can be great fun.

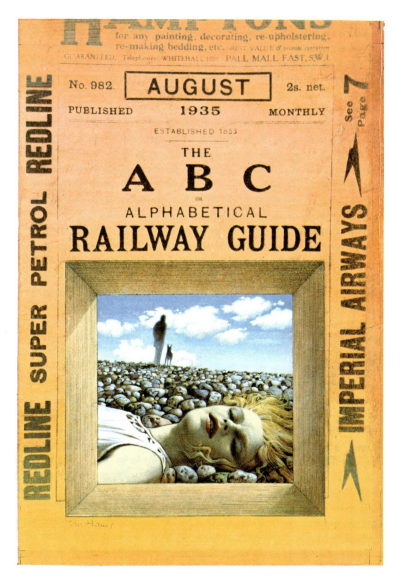

THE ABC MURDERS (U.S. version)

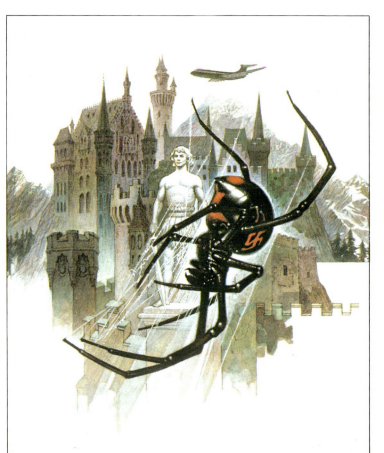

PASSENGER TO FRANKFURT

JULIAN SYMONS
A late book, a weak book, but a fine cover. The story has a flavour both Wagnerian and Gothic, and this is caught in the Bavarian schloss, in those mostly unpleasant and highly Teutonic faces, and in the skull that separates them.

TOM ADAMS
For the first version of this story, the female villain is represented by the black widow spider at the centre of her web. The statue is of the Wagnerian hero, Siegfried and the background castle is based on that outrageous piece of fairy tale fantasy, Neuschwanstein Castle.

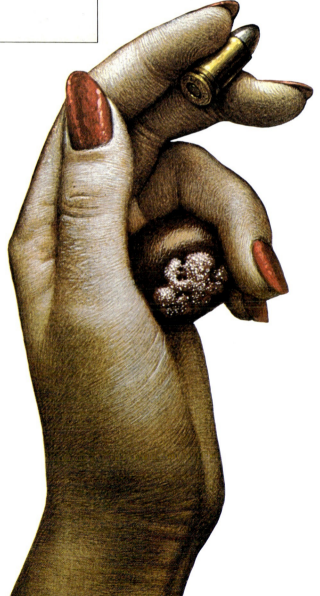

THE BIG FOUR

JULIAN SYMONS
This was written in the Twenties, shortly after Agatha Christie's separation from her husband Archie. It was conceived as four short stories. Then they were stitched together so that the joins don't show except on careful examination, and the whole was turned into one of those stories about world domination by a gang to which the author occasionally, and unhappily, turned. One of the Big Four is (but of course!) Chinese, and he is symbolised by the rich and splendid dragon. The chess piece is a vital element in one of the stories. The cover does the book more than justice.

TOM ADAMS
The chess piece is one of the bishops in the now famous walrus ivory set excavated on the island of Lewis, off the West Coast of Scotland.

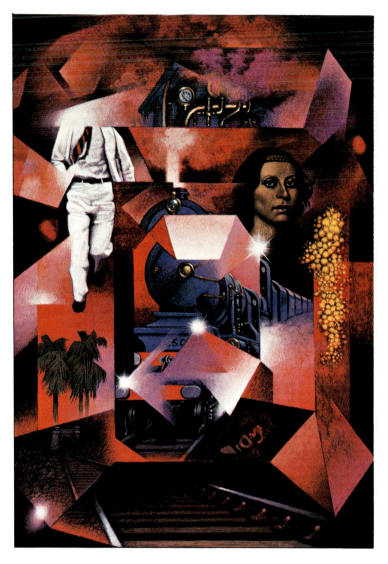

MYSTERY OF THE BLUE TRAIN

TOM ADAMS
An early story, apparently Christie's least favourite but not as bad as all that. The train detail comes from the American version and in the English version, I gave myself the problem of disposing elements of the story amongst the facets of a ruby without breaking up the image too much.

MURDER ON THE ORIENT EXPRESS (U.S.) MURDER ON THE CALAIS COACH

JULIAN SYMONS
Which actor has given us the best Poirot? I saw the very first of them, the eminent Charles Laughton, in *Alibi* (a splendid performance, but of course Laughton was physically quite unsuited to the part), and most of the others, including Austin Trevor in several films of the Thirties, and more recently Peter Ustinov in *Death on the Nile*. For my money, Albert Finney's performance in *Murder on the Orient Express* was outstanding. He managed uncannily the physical resemblance, down to the suspiciously black hair and the head slightly to one side, he was eccentric but conveyed acute intelligence, his movements and gestures were just right. A masterly performance: Agatha Christie should have been, and was, pleased with it.

Because of her love affair with trains ("it is sad nowadays that one no longer has engines that seem to be one's personal friends") she must also have loved the opening of this film, the train standing at the station, engine wreathed in steam, with the star-studded cast coming down the platform to board it. . . .

How does one give the reader a taste of the story's romantic feeling, and its complexity, while avoiding the conventional cliches of a train puffing through an exotic landscape, or of a much-stabbed body? The artist's solution is beautifully simple. A small section of a survey map of Macedonia as background, and on it a selection from the confusing clues, the dented watch saying 1.15, the burnt matches, the pipe cleaner, the charred bit of paper. I have rarely seen a cover that suggested mysterious things so well, yet so perfectly avoided the obvious.

TOM ADAMS
Certainly one of the best known and most admired of Christies. I might well have used a train as part of the illustration but in the English version, I resisted the temptation. It was only after a great deal of abortive research into the magnificent Orient Express

interiors and my failure to come up with any really satisfactory reference in the time available, that I reluctantly decided to scrap the idea. I am not entirely happy with this painting, particularly as the watch looks remarkably unbattered. Let's be charitable and suggest it is very badly damaged on the back!

◀ MURDER IN MESOPOTAMIA

TOM ADAMS
The first and the most specifically archaeological of all those stories of Agatha Christie's which were set in or around her beloved Middle Eastern digging grounds. Not, I fear, a very profound cover but I enjoyed making the plasticine mask and it is one of several paintings in which I tackled the task of depicting rope, whiskers and all.

DEATH ON THE NILE ▶

JULIAN SYMONS
Admirably emblematic, this cover, giving away nothing of the puzzle, yet showing us the revolver that is at the heart of the story, since it is used in the shooting of Simon Doyle. The effect of the inscrutable head behind the revolver is enhanced by obscuring one eye. The sensational possibilities of the theme are avoided in a quite masterly way.

TOM ADAMS
This is really a very simple basic formula cover except that I was interested in trying an unusual perspective view of that strange little pearl-handled revolver, with the fold-away trigger.

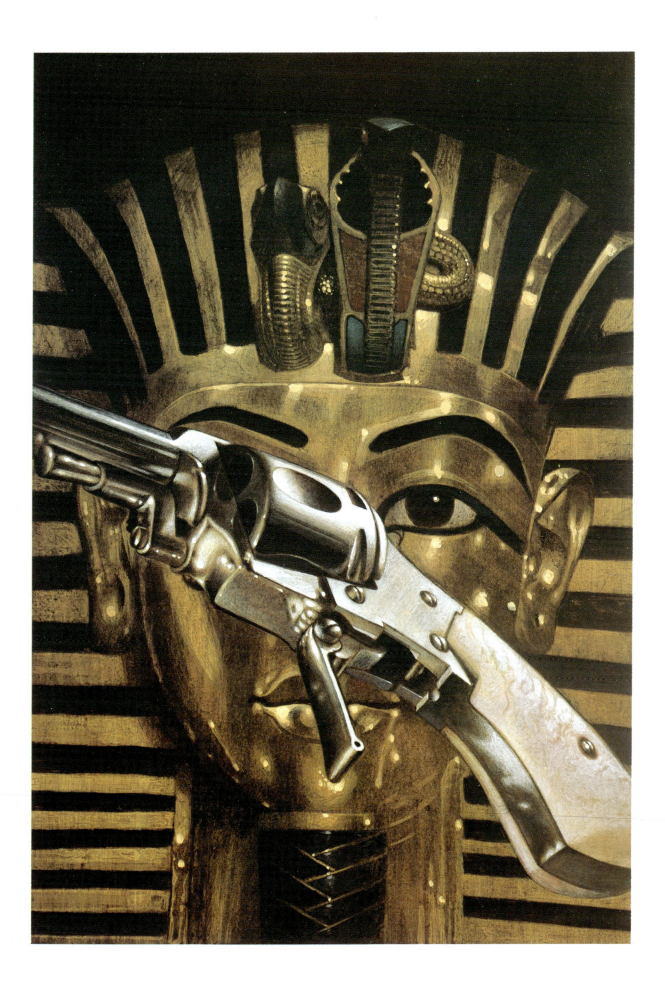

APPOINTMENT WITH DEATH

JULIAN SYMONS
Spellbinding, I call this one. The spider
emerging from the head of a beautiful girl
and, as it seems, about to crawl down over
her face, symbolises—just what, exactly?
For the sake of the story's future readers it
is not possible to say more, not even about
the identity of the girl. As an image of
impending evil, this cover could hardly be
bettered. You need not be an arachnophobe
to find it terrifying. The effect of the spider
is a little like that of the rats confronting
Winston Smith in *1984*.

TOM ADAMS
I have always been fascinated by spiders.
After conquering an early childhood fear I
have occasionally kept them as pets, mated
them and raised their enormous families.
This is basically the trap door spider
(Pachylomerides Nitidularis) with some
liberties taken.
    The symbol is perhaps a touch obscure
but the face is meant to be ambiguous. The
girl is enmeshed in evil. But as perpetrator
or victim? You will have to read the book
to find out.

◄ DESTINATION UNKNOWN ►
(U.S.) SO MANY STEPS TO DEATH

JULIAN SYMONS
A perfect example of the artist interpreting
a book's theme in terms of his own macabre
romantic images, while remaining faithful
to the author's theme. The painting owes, a
lot to Dali, Tom Adams says, and I though
something to Tanguy as well, yet the result
is original. The effects are mysterious and
sinister, the background rocks turning into
the foreground toad, the half-hooded leper,
the trail of balls leading back across the
desert. As a painting this seems to me one
of the finest in the series, and every one of
the elements it contains can be justified by
reference to the book. The difference? The
book is often light, almost flippant, it
contains little of the atmosphere expressed
in the cover. A rather average Christie has
generated a genuine work of art.

TOM ADAMS
An illustration inspired by classic surrealism;
Dali being the main source as Magritte is in
the second version of *Murder at the Vicarage*
   Perhaps the very act of explaining this
blatant eclecticism will seem like an
apology but I must risk that. I consider it a
perfectly legitimate practice for an illustrator
occasionally to borrow the clothes of well
known artists; indeed it is not altogether
unknown in the realms of the so called Fine
Arts. In particular it is fairly obvious that
the classical surrealism of Dali and
Magritte lends itself admirably to the
symbolist illustration of thrillers and crime
stories.
   The earlier version is a very dated
psychedelic sixties illustration. It was one
of my first attempts to break out of the still
life straightjacket I had fashioned for
myself. There were other occasional stylistic
breaks for freedom; some more, some less
successful.

A CARIBBEAN MYSTERY

JULIAN SYMONS

Miss Marple has met many old soldiers, some handsome upright figures, others "regrettably unattractive; and Major Palgrave, purple of face, with a glass eye, and the general appearance of a stuffed frog, belonged in the latter category". Here in the first version is Major Palgrave, a horrific image. What his glass eye sees (or fails to see) is vitally important to the story, but both in this and in the second version where the blood-veined glass eye looks down like the sun upon a dead girl, the artist has worked very successfully against the grain of the story. This applies especially to the second version, in which the deliberate overblown romanticism seems derived in part from the pre-Raphaelites and in part from the Douanier Rousseau. It is as though the artist said: "Enough of Miss Marple's cosiness. We are in the South Seas, and I am going to render their lushness and perversity, together with the undertone of witchcraft". The result is two remarkable paintings, the details of which are totally faithful to events in the story.

TOM ADAMS

In both these covers I feel I have been as Julian Symons says "totally faithful" to the actual story and also produced paintings which make beguiling covers. In other words for me at least, they are both successful. It is interesting that the Christie family later told me how much they disliked the first version. I suppose the horror of the glass eye which has popped out of Major Palgrave's dead face was too much for them. But I find it at least equally amusing as horrifying and what's wrong with a touch of the *grand guignol* now and then? I have found that most people's inclination is to laugh rather than scream at my covers. The laugh might be a nervous giggle or end in a shiver but that, as far as I am concerned, is the perfect reaction.

In this second version of *A Caribbean Mystery* there is a parallel with *The ABC Murders*, in which a dead girl seems to blend with or melt into the surrounding elements—a theme I find intriguing. I love this painting. Regretfully I now no longer own the originals of this or the American *ABC Murders*.

DEATH COMES AS THE END
(U.S. version)

TOM ADAMS
The commentaries on this American version
are in Chapter 3.

CHAPTER SEVEN

A MIXED BAG

"We will hunt down murderers, and discover
the missing family jewels, and find people
who've disappeared and detect embezzlers."
Tuppence (*Partners in Crime*)

Apart from the fact that this last section of the book contains five short story collections, as the title implies, there are no real themes. Perhaps one could sub-title it, 'a miscellaneous assortment of detectives' such as Parker Pyne, Harley Quin, Tommy and Tuppence, Inspector Battle and Colonel Race. They are rather an odd lot in some ways but, being a romantic at heart, I have a soft spot for Harley Quin and I don't think Tommy and Tuppence are quite as obnoxious as some critics suggest. It is really only their names which are faintly nauseating. I rather feel that as time elapses and the twenties acquire even more of a period charm than they have now, these two typical products of that flippant decade will become more acceptable.

The two recent British television films *Why Didn't They Ask Evans?* and the much better *Seven Dials Mystery* were successful examples of how entertaining even the slightest of tales can be with delicious period props, clothes and cars; the hats that Cheryl Campbell wore as Lady Eileen 'Bundle' Brent were divine, as indeed Miss Campbell was herself.

There is more than a whiff of the occult in this section; *The Mysterious Mr Quin* and *The Hound of Death* are full of it. The last two books are light-hearted romps — Agatha Christie in festive mood with Poirot and Miss Marple in *The Adventure of a Christmas Pudding* and *Partners in Crime* with the Tommy and Tuppence due.

As this is the final chapter of the book, I will say something in general about the work I have carried out over about eighteen years on these paintings. As you can no doubt imagine, having produced well over a hundred paintings for Christie covers (they are not all reproduced in this book), it has occasionally, only quite rarely in fact, been a chore. Not all of these stories have inspired me and I hope I have been honest enough to admit this when it has happened. In the main, however, it has been a labour of love.

There is something about Agatha Christie stories, journeyman writer though she may have been, which trigger my imagination. I shall ever be deeply grateful to her.

In ending with two final quotations, the last one from Professor Robert Barnard's excellent book on Agatha Christie, I would like to acknowledge my debt to him in writing these introductory pieces. After reading and illustrating Christie for nearly twenty years, I have accumulated some knowledge on my subject but his clear-headed and affectionate assessments were invaluable to me in tidying up my own ideas.

"If I could write like Elizabeth Bowen, Muriel Spark or Graham Greene, I would jump to high heaven with delight, but I know I can't."

Agatha Christie — *An Autobiography*

"And if she had no desire to elevate her 'trade' into a 'profession' by writing anything that could be confused with a 'real novel', still less was she bitten by the fine-writing bug . . . The main characteristic of Agatha Christie's writing is that one does not notice it. And that, perhaps, is about the highest praise one could give to a writer of popular literature."

A Talent to Deceive by Robert Barnard

◀ THE SEVEN DIALS MYSTERY

JULIAN SYMONS
Early, and emphatically Grade 2 Christie—
to put it kindly—a preposterous story about
a society of crime fighters who call
themselves the Seven Dials and wear clock
masks with the hour hand pointing at
numbers from 1 to 7. What can an artist do
with such material? Well, here's a powerful
design of a gloved hand holding a gun, and
in the background (just count) seven dials.

TOM ADAMS
Not much to say about this except that the
hand and the glove are mine and, therefore,
the killer (as I am right-handed) had to be
left-handed; or alternatively, is this just
another Christie mirror image? It is a
misleading cover, in no way evoking the
fairly light-hearted romp this story is.

THE MYSTERIOUS MR. QUIN ▶

JULIAN SYMONS
The stories about Mr. Harley Quin are
favourites of Tom Adams, although not of
mine. This cover, one in a second batch
commissioned after *A Murder is Announced*
had been approved, shows a developing
subtlety. The background is from the copy
of a seventeenth century drawing showing
Harlequin and Columbine, the revolver was
pinned to the drawing for working
purposes, and the death's head moth is a
symbolic touch, expressing what the artist
calls the magic and mystery in the tales.

TOM ADAMS
My reasons for liking Mr. Quin are hard to
pin down. Generally speaking I think
Christie is underrated as a short story writer
and, although the Harley Quin stories are
not by any means her best, they have a
certain whimsical mysticism I find attractive.

Just as the goat/man element many years
later in *Murder is Easy* has connections
with *The Magus* by John Fowles, so this
cover is quite simply another version of my
painting for *The Collector*, Fowles' first
published novel, the cover for which was
instrumental in triggering the whole
Christie series.

I tried hard in this one to convey the
contrast between the hard cold brutality of
the dark gun metal with the velvety
softness of the death's head hawk moth.
The revolver was borrowed from a friend
and featured in several of my cover
paintings, the latest of which is *Elephants
Can Remember*.

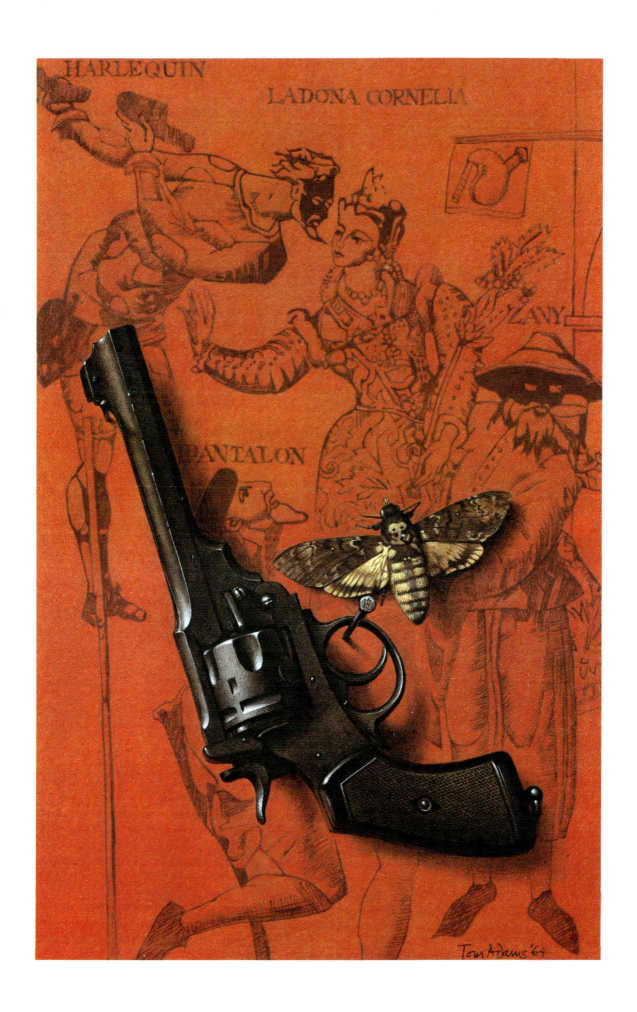

◄ PARKER PYNE INVESTIGATES (U.S.) MR. PARKER PYNE, DETECTIVE

JULIAN SYMONS
Mr. Parker Pyne was a character never used except in this collection of stories, although he had that element of the uncanny about him which appealed to Agatha Christie. Nothing much to say about the cover, except that the medal is nicely painted.

TOM ADAMS
The original of this painting is in Canada and, in spite of Julian's dismissive comment, I consider it as one of the finest I ever did. I never again managed to blend the two dimensional and thrice dimensional imagery with quite such subtelty—probably pure luck. To be fair to Julian, however, he only saw a small transparency.

N OR M? ►

JULIAN SYMONS
A wartime thriller with Nazi spies lurking in or around a seaside guest house where Poirot goes to stay. Inferior Christie, with little to inspire the artist, but out of various elements he has made an ingenious design, with its background of sand. The bloody hammer with hairs sticking to it is what really catches the attention.

TOM ADAMS
Another *grand-guignol* favourite of Mark Collins. Cow gum, red paint and real human hair did the trick here, combined with a laborious painting of sand. Compare this with the English version of *Evil Under the Sun*.

SPARKLING CYANIDE
(U.S.) REMEMBERED DEATH

JULIAN SYMONS
What's the ornamental evening bag doing there, along with the cyanide and the glass of champagne into which the cyanide was tipped? Symbolism again. Effective and comparatively straightforward, the European cover is the work of an artist feeling his way.

The American one, which I should suppose to have been done later, uses surrealism brilliantly in posing the static, formal figure holding the champagne glass against the two background women, with the whole complicated and made more subtle by the obscuring branches in the foreground.

The murder took place at a dinner party, and evening bags would obviously have been used.

TOM ADAMS
By the time I did the Fontana version of this I was well into my stride as a still life painter and I had begun to learn the importance of simplicity both in design and content. A lesson which I subsequently forgot on several occasions, to my cost.

The delicate texture of the little embroidered evening bag was a challenge I enjoyed.

The American edition is interesting in that although I was under a strict injunction to paint very realistic covers for them, I pushed this one a long way towards a graphic simplicity.

The 'obscuring branches' in the foreground are in fact rosemary twigs. Another example of the exaggerated perspective technique.

REMEMBERED DEATH

◀ PARTNERS IN CRIME

TOM ADAMS
This is a book of short stories, being the awfully jolly pranks of the amateur sleuths Tommy and Tuppence parodying the styles of famous detectives, from Sherlock Holmes to Poirot himself. Lightweight stuff with a lightweight cover to match.

ADVENTURES OF THE ▶ CHRISTMAS PUDDING

JULIAN SYMONS
An unusually jolly cover this, in which the artist has altogether caught the feeling of the title story in the collection of two long and four short tales. Somebody is playing jokes on Poirot, like telling him not to touch the Christmas pudding—or are they jokes? Can they be, when young Bridget is found lying dead in the snow? No more must be said, no secret must be given away, but—yes, this is a Christmas story, and the jollity of the cover is altogether appropriate. A nice change from the sinister.

TOM ADAMS
In some ways a jolly cover but surely the robin redbreast is a touch sinister—more Transylvanian than traditional, perhaps?

The green cover is a very early one in which one is reminded of those palmy days when Christmas puddings were filled with real sixpences, shillings and lucky charms.

◀ ADVENTURES OF THE CHRISTMAS PUDDING

THE HOUND OF DEATH ▶

JULIAN SYMONS
A woman who dreams about the City of Crystal, another woman who tries to recapture here dead child when a medium evokes it in ectoplasm, a girl with four distinct personalities—Agatha Christie's interest in unknowable worlds strongly colours this collection. The crystal ball with the seeing eye is a finely conceived counterpart to the other-worldly atmosphere of the tales.

TOM ADAMS
I borrowed the skull from an artist acquaintance and I remember distinctly how reluctant he was to part with it and acutely nervous about me having it in my studio. He used to telephone me almost every day to ask how it was and much too soon to ask for it back. I understood his possessiveness completely, it was a particularly beautiful skull. Although this was only my second Christie cover and done therefore many years ago, I vividly recall my enormous satisfaction in painting it. I also remember the almost childlike enthusiasm the painting received from Mark Collins, Virgil Pomfret and Christine Bernard, the then art director at Collins— bless their hearts. Those were heady days at Fontana. I used the same skull later in *The Hallowe'en Party*.

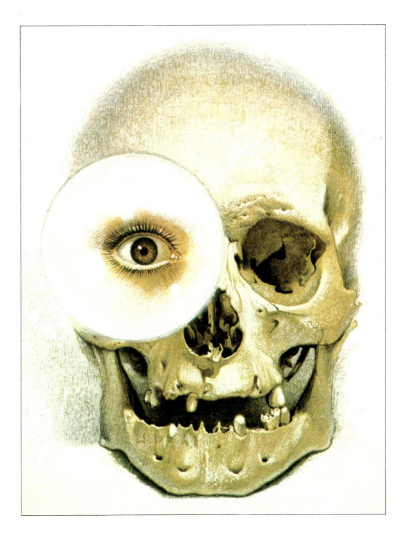

BY THE PRICKING OF MY THUMBS
(U.S. version)

JULIAN SYMONS
The American cover for this story is rich
with romantic gloom. The hand holding the
slightly overblown rose, the skull on the
side of the tomb, the bird, the sad trees,
the background figures, all these combine
to make what is, irrespective of its relationship to the book, a fine romantic painting.

TOM ADAMS
This version for the American paperback
imprint, Pocket Books, combines a grave
from a small Hampstead churchyard with
some tombstones from a vast cemetery
near Wimbledon Common where I used to
walk every day with my dogs when in
London.
   I pulled the hand with the rose from the
background into the foreground. The rose
is a 'Commandant Beaurepaire' or York and
Lancaster rose mentioned in the book. The
suggestive blood red splashes of this
marvellous old-fashioned rose were a gift.

140

THE CASE OF THE
MISSING PAINTINGS

The 8 original paintings, titled here, have
mysteriously disappeared.

Cat Among the Pigeons
Cards on the Table
The Crooked House (European version)
Towards Zero (European version)
Endless Night (any of three versions!)
By the Pricking of My Thumbs (Second
European version)

Any information as to the whereabouts of these
sadly missed originals will be gratefully received.

INDEX

We gratefully acknowledge the permission
granted by Collins to quote from various
works by Agatha Christie and from her
Autobiography and also by Dodd, Mead
& Co for quotations from A Talent to
Deceive by Robert Barnard.

LIST OF OWNERS

The ABC Murders (European version)	The Geoffrey Greenwood Collection
The ABC Murders (U.S. version)	Collection Dr & Mrs G.K. Bohlig
Adventures of the Christmas Pudding	Collection Elizabeth Hamilton
And Then There Were None (European version)	The Geoffrey Greenwood Collection
Appointment with Death	Collection G.E. Dagendorfer
At Bertram's Hotel	The Geoffrey Greenwood Collection
The Big Four	The Geoffrey Greenwood Collection
The Body in the Library (European version)	The Geoffrey Greenwood Collection
By the Pricking of my Thumbs (First version)	The Geoffrey Greenwood Collection
By the Pricking of my Thumbs (U.S. version)	The Geoffrey Greenwood Collection
A Caribbean Mystery (First version)	The Geoffrey Greenwood Collection
A Caribbean Mystery (Second version)	Collection Dr & Mrs B. Schachter
The Crooked House (U.S. version)	The Geoffrey Greenwood Collection
Dean Man's Folly (European version)	The Geoffrey Greenwood Collection
Death Comes as the End (European version)	Collection Mr & Mrs Craig
Death Comes as the End (U.S. version)	Collection Rudolph Vogelsanger
Death in the Clouds	The Geoffrey Greenwood Collection
Destination Unknown (First version)	The Geoffrey Greenwood Collection
Elephants Can Remember	Collection Rudolph Vogelsanger
Evil Under the Sun (U.S. version)	Collection Tom Gorrie
Five Little Pigs	Collection Mrs Sobell
The 4.50 from Paddington	Collection Lucinda Vardey
Hallowe'en Party	The Geoffrey Greenwood Collection
Hercule Poirot's Christmas	The Geoffrey Greenwood Collection
Hercule Poirot's Christmas (Second version)	Collection David Hamilton
Hickory Dickory Dock	Collection Sharon Budd
Hickory Dickory Dock (U.S. version)	Collection Mr & Mrs Surinder Bhatia
The Hollow	The Geoffrey Greenwood Collection
The Hound of Death	The Geoffrey Greenwood Collection
Lord Edgeware Dies	The Jan Pienkowski Collection
The Mirror Crack'd from Side to Side	The Jan Pienkowski Collection
Murder at the Vicarage	Collection Charlotte Adams
Murder at the Vicarage (Second version)	Collection Mr & Mrs W. Ross Degeer
A Murder is Announced	The Geoffrey Greenwood Collection
The Murder of Roger Ackroyd	The Geoffrey Greenwood Collection
Murder on the Orient Express	The Geoffrey Greenwood Collection
Mystery of the Blue Train (European version)	Collection Mr & Mrs M. Alexander
One Two Buckle My Shoe	The Geoffrey Greenwood Collection
Ordeal by Innocence (Two European versions)	The Geoffrey Greenwood Collection
The Pale Horse	The Geoffrey Greenwood Collection
Parker Pyne Investigates	Collection Mark Lang
Passenger to Frankfurt (Second version)	Collection Mr & Mrs Ron MacFeeters
Peril at End House	Collection Mr & Mrs M. Alexander
A Pocket Full of Rye	The Asger Jerrild Collection
Postern of Fate	Collection Dr Walker
The Sittaford Mystery	The Geoffrey Greenwood Collection
Sleeping Murder	Collection Mr & Mrs Surinder Bhatia
They Do It With Mirrors	Collection Jonathan Adams